Thomas Wentworth Higginson, Maria E. MacKaye

The Abbess of Port Royal and other French Studies

Thomas Wentworth Higginson, Maria E. MacKaye

The Abbess of Port Royal and other French Studies

ISBN/EAN: 9783337243715

Printed in Europe, USA, Canada, Australia, Japan

Cover: Foto ©ninafisch / pixelio.de

More available books at **www.hansebooks.com**

THE ABBESS OF PORT ROYAL

AND

OTHER FRENCH STUDIES

BY

MARIA ELLERY MACKAYE

WITH AN INTRODUCTION

BY

THOMAS WENTWORTH HIGGINSON

BOSTON
LEE AND SHEPARD PUBLISHERS
10 MILK STREET
1892

COPYRIGHT, 1891, BY MARIA ELLERY MACKAYE.

All Rights Reserved.

THE ABBESS OF PORT ROYAL AND OTHER FRENCH STUDIES.

TYPOGRAPHY AND ELECTROTYPING BY
C. J. PETERS & SON, BOSTON.

PRESS OF ROCKWELL & CHURCHILL, BOSTON.

INTRODUCTION

WE sometimes see the remark made, that while American women are making large contributions to poetry and fiction, they are not yet doing their full share of thoughtful and studious literary work. Such a volume as the present helps to refute that criticism. Many years of enlightened study, both in this country and Paris, have helped to mature the execution and broaden the background of these French stories. Most of the essays have appeared in the *Atlantic Monthly*, the *Galaxy*, or elsewhere; and the repeated demand at our college libraries — for instance, at Harvard — for the detached papers has resulted in the publication in this collected form.

The present writer recalls with a certain pleasure the fact that one of the most attractive of these papers — that entitled "Provençal Song" — appeared originally, through a misapprehension, with his name attached to it as author; he having been merely the medium of communication between the real writer and the editor of the *Galaxy*. He now regrets that the statement was not correct.

THOMAS WENTWORTH HIGGINSON.

CAMBRIDGE, MASS., Aug. 1, 1891.

CONTENTS

	PAGE
THE ABBESS OF PORT ROYAL	1
THE SONG OF ROLAND	44
BEAUMARCHAIS	65
FRENCH WOMEN BEFORE THE REVOLUTION	93
"THE MARVELS OF MONT SAINT MICHEL"	115
PROVENCAL SONG	129

THE ABBESS OF PORT ROYAL

Qui ne connaît pas Port Royal, ne connaît pas l'humanité. — ROYER-COLLARD.

FRENCH Protestantism in the sixteenth century, according to Sainte-Beuve, was the work of the aristocracy, or at least of the gentry. Port Royal was the religious expression of the best part of the middle classes in France.

In 1599, the last year of the sixteenth century, little Jacqueline Arnauld, a child of seven, was appointed coadjutrix to the lady abbess of Port Royal, while her sister Jeanne, two years younger, was made abbess of the neighboring convent of Saint Cyr. Antoine Arnauld, father of these children, and of a numerous progeny besides, was an eminent lawyer of Huguenot descent; and their grandfather, M. Marion, advocate-general of Henry IV., was a favorite of that monarch, who was not very strict, as we know, in his ideas about abbeys and sacraments. He probably considered this a legitimate and honorable method of providing for the younger daughters of his friends. The Pope's bull, however, confirming these appointments, was not forthcoming. Antoine Arnauld had made a great reputation by a famous plea against the Jesuits, instrumental in procuring their recent expulsion. His courageous eloquence had won from the University of France an official expression of everlasting gratitude, but it had also secured to him the undying hatred of the "Order," and of his friends at court. Everything went on as if the confirmation had been issued in due form. Little Jeanne went to Saint Cyr to perform her duties by proxy, and Jacqueline was sent away from home to a convent, to be trained for her new responsibilities, and to be initiated into her religious life. The choice of abode was a strange one, for she was sent to Maubuisson.

Midway between Creil and Paris, on the Chemin du fer du Nord, near the station of Saint-Ouen-l'Aumône, where you change cars for Dieppe, rise the ruins of this stately abbey, founded by Blanche, mother of Saint Louis. Here Jacqueline dwelt for two years, under the care and guidance of Madame Angélique d'Estrées, Abbess of Maubuisson and Bertaumont, the unworthy sister of the far-famed Gabrielle. At first, Madame d'Estrées had only presided over the Abbey of Bertaumont, near Amiens, where Henry IV. was a frequent visitor. It is said that Gabrielle complained of being banished so far from Paris, and begged her royal lover to give her sister charge of some other convent not so remote. So the abbess of Maubuisson was notified that another would be appointed in her stead, and the king signified his wishes, convoked the chapter in person, and installed Madame Angélique and her fair sister in their new domain. Thus, in the shadow of the royal amours, and under the influence of such a woman, Jacqueline passed two years of her childhood and received her first impressions of convent life. Once, during this period, she accompanied the abbess on a visit to Maubuisson, was confirmed there, and took Madame d'Estrées' own name, Angélique. The old abbess of Port Royal had just died, and a new nomination was to be sent to Rome, no longer of Jacqueline Arnauld, as coadjutrix, but of Angélique Arnauld, as abbess, and her age was stated as seventeen, when, in fact, she was hardly nine years old. Even then difficulties were made, and, only after a great deal of adroit diplomacy in support of the falsehood, the Pope's consent was obtained, and the bull issued, investing Angélique with the dignity of the abbess of the monastery of Port Royal, where she now took up her abode, after being regularly installed in presence of an august assemblage.

The abbey of Port Royal des Champs, about eighteen miles to the west of Paris, lies in a narrow valley, completely shut in by wooded hills. It was founded in the year 1204, by Eudes de Sully, Bishop of Paris, and Mathilde de Garlande, who had made a vow for the salvation and safe return of her husband, a crusader with Foulques de Neuilly. The name is said to come from the Low Latin word *borra* or *porra*, signifying a hole full of brambles and stagnant water, only too descriptive of the original state of the valley. Twelve years after its foundation it was called " Portu-Regio," thus sanctioning the legend of Philip-Augustus, who, having lost his way in the chase, took refuge in a little chapel dedicated to Saint Laurence on this spot, and founded the abbey in grateful recognition of the shelter afforded, thence called Port Royal. So says tradition, but historical records do not confirm the story.

The convent belonged to the Order of Saint Bernard; but some of the first nuns were Benedictines, and they were under the supervision of the monks of Citeaux, at the neighboring convent of Vaux de Cernay, now a picturesque and imposing ruin, belonging to Madame Nathaniel Rothschild. Vaux de Cernay was founded in 1128, by

Simon de Montfort, also a patron and benefactor of Port Royal. Thibaut, grandson of Mathilde de Garlande, became the abbot of Vauxde Cernay, and evidently regarded with great favor the convent near by, founded by his grandmother. During the visits he made to Port Royal as superior, he inhabited a small detached building near the porter's lodge that ever after went by his name.

Four hundred years had passed away since Mathilde de Garlande kept her pious vow, when the child abbess came into possession of her new domain, no longer a stagnant fen, but a fair and fertile valley, embosoming a goodly convent. The rule had been very much relaxed, as was generally the case at that period, and more or less disorder prevailed, though the epitaph of the old abbess, who had lately died, recorded that "she had not neglected her convent, and had fed her nuns well." At the time of the accession of Mère Angélique, the confessor was an ignorant old monk, who did not understand his "Pater," could not say one word of the catechism, and never opened a book but his breviary. There had been no preaching at Port Royal for the last thirty years, except on the rare occasions when a nun took the veil. They went to communion once a month and on high feast days, always excepting that of the purification, that came in carnival time when all the house was in confusion, and the confessor and the nuns had as much as they could do to prepare for masquerades. The sisters followed the fashion of wearing masks and gloves to preserve their complexions. There were only thirteen nuns in all, and the eldest, thirty-three years old, was soon sent away by Madame Arnauld for unseemly conduct. The young abbess led a regular life and conducted all the services, beginning

with the matins at four o'clock. The rest of the time she
played or rambled about the place, attending particularly
to one of the regulations that directed the lady abbess to
take the community to walk after vespers. Rainy days
she read romances, or the history of Rome, by way of
recreation. The prioress attended to all the material
wants of the house. There was not much luxury, for they
were not rich and the servants were wasteful, but there
was a great deal of liberty in private expenditure, and
some of the nuns had their own furniture and silver service. The Arnauld family exercised a vigilant oversight,
Madame Arnauld, especially, often arriving from Paris unexpectedly; but all was quiet and orderly, and the general
of the Order, on his annual visit of inspection, pronounced
everything satisfactory, and increased the number of nuns
to sixteen. One day Henry IV., hunting in the neighborhood, called at the abbey to see Antoine Arnauld, Angélique's father, then on a visit to the convent, during the
parliamentary recess. The youthful abbess went out in
great state, at the head of all her nuns, to meet the king.
She was mounted for the occasion on high-heeled over-
shoes, and the king complimented her on being tall for
her age. He promised to come back and dine the next
day, but the hunt taking him in another direction, he sent
his excuses in due form, and then shouted as he passed
close under the walls, on horseback, "The king kisses
the hands of the lady abbess." This was his first and last
visit to Port Royal; little else occurred to break the mo-
notony, and after five long years Angélique grew weary of
a life that began to inspire her with disgust. She confided in no one, however, and when people suggested that
she was not bound by vows made when she was a minor,

she never appeared to entertain the idea, and discouraged such remarks. She began, however, to make and receive visits, proceedings that interfered with the regularity of convent life, and displeased her mother, who did not spare remonstrances and exhortations. Angélique saw at last that she must submit to the rule, or else afflict her parents and do discredit to her position. She gave up her excursions, and tried for a time to console herself by reading "Plutarch's Lives," and other profane books ; but, in spite of this diversion, her life grew so intolerable that she meditated escape, dreamed of marriage, and seriously planned taking refuge with her Huguenot aunts at La Rochelle. On the eve of carrying out this design, she fell ill, probably from nervous excitement, and was taken home on a litter. She was tenderly cared for in her father's house in Paris, and on her recovery, the affectionate child had lost the courage to distress those who loved her by such a scandal. It is possible that in her delirium she may have betrayed her secret ; at all events, one day, soon after her recovery, her father surprised her by suddenly presenting an illegibly written page, laying it before her, and saying in a peremptory tone, "Sign this, my daughter, there, in that place," pointing out the spot for the signature. One glance convinced her that it was a confirmation of her vows, but she did not dare to resist, and wrote her name, "ready to die with shame and anger," as she said afterwards. Disheartened and humiliated by this trick, still feeble from severe and prolonged illness, she returned disconsolately to Port Royal and the hated convent-life ; but the glad welcome of the nuns, who had feared to lose her, made her a little more reconciled to what she began to regard as an inevitable fate. During the following Lent, wanting a book to read, and afraid to ask for profane literature, she took up a volume of meditations, left by a Capuchin monk at the convent, thought it beautiful, and found it consoling.

While this comforting impression was still vivid, a Capuchin presented himself one night at the convent-gate, asking permission to preach. They had just returned from the walk after vespers, and Mère Angélique at first refused on account of the lateness of the hour, but finally consented, and the sisters gathered in the church to hear the sermon. Any change was a welcome relief from the wretched preaching of the students from Citeaux, who usually officiated at Port Royal, and this service at the close of day was a variety. The monk took for his subject the humility of the Son of God, and his birth in the manger. Mère Angélique never remembered distinctly what he said; but during the sermon her heart was touched so that all at once her condition seemed as glorious as it had till then appeared grievous, and she rejoiced, instead of sorrowing, at the irrevocable nature of her vows. This hour of her life was the first gleam that broadened later into the perfect day. It would have seemed a natural impulse to confide in the man whose sermon had been the occasion of this miraculous change; but with characteristic dignity the girl of fifteen sent one of the sisters to thank the monk and to speed him on his way. Afterwards it was known that he was a most disreputable character, who had been already a cause of scandal in several communities. An older man, the austere Père Bernard, was taken into her confidence and consulted in regard to the various reforms that she now began to feel it her bounden duty to make. This Capuchin was very injudicious, however, and aroused at once the violent opposition of the best and most religious of the nuns, who felt aggrieved by his wholesale denunciations of their quiet lives. He drew up a set of new regulations in strict conformity with the old Benedictine rule, and submitted them to the prior of Citeaux, in spite of the urgent remonstrance of Mère Angélique, who knew the prior well, and was sure that he would disapprove and complain to her father. The laxity of this dignitary may be inferred from the fact that he had recently been present at a theatrical entertainment given by " Les Dames de Saint Antoine." The play was the " Cleopatra " of Garnier, and the nuns were dressed in men's clothes for the male parts. Other distinguished ecclesiastics were also present, and the abbess was no less a person than Mademoiselle de Thou, sister of the president and aunt of the historian of that name. In spite of this array of respectable laxity, reform was counselled by the Capuchin advisers of Mère Angélique. One monk, Père Pacifique, sympathized with her ardent desire to go away, no longer into the world to get married, but as a lay sister to some other convent of stricter rule. Père Bernard, however, insisted that she should stay where she was and reform Port Royal. A whole year went by, troubled by interior and exterior conflict. At times God seemed to veil his face again, and there was a constant struggle with the nuns, who thought their young abbess unreasonable and extravagant, and who strenuously opposed all her plans. She had recourse in secret to the greatest austerities, deprived herself of food and rest, dropped burning wax upon her bare arms, and committed other follies that she was the first to blame in after years ; but, as she said, "I tried everything then." Madame Juneauville, one of the nuns, employed by her mother to watch her, slept in her cell for that purpose; but when it was dark Mère Angélique would often creep softly away into a garret and spend the night in prayer. Warned, as she had foreseen, by the prior, M. Arnauld arrived one day unexpectedly, drove away all the Capuchin advisers with expressions of contempt and dislike, and carried his daughter off to his château of Andilly to enjoy the season of vintage. But home was no longer charming to her; her father condemned all her plans of reform, and she returned to Port Royal as soon as he would allow her to do so, ill with intermittent fever and very unhappy. One day a student from Citeaux preached on the text, "Blessed are they who are persecuted for righteousness' sake." After the sermon one of the girls employed as a domestic in the convent said to her, "Madame, if you chose, you might be one of those blessed ones." Mère Angélique rebuked the girl for her boldness, but the words sank into her heart.

Not long after, she took occasion to renew her vows publicly, and made a solemn declaration of her resolve to lead in future a truly religious life. Some of the sisters followed her example; but she saw no way of accomplishing her reforms, and despondently recurred at times to her plan of going, as a lay sister, to another convent. One day the prioress sought an interview and inquired the cause of her great melancholy; learning the reason that she no doubt divined, she told her that the sisters wished her to say that they preferred to accede to her wishes to seeing her so ill and depressed, and that they would oppose her no longer. Unspeakably rejoiced, she at once appointed a day, convoked the chapter, and proposed community of goods in accordance with the first vow of poverty. The sisters at once agreed, and brought all their possessions, even their clothing, to swell the common fund. One, however, could not give up her little garden. The next step was to enforce the sanctity of the cloister, to shut the world out from the convent. Mère Angélique felt that she herself must set the example, and determined to allow no exceptions, not even in the persons of her immediate family. At Easter, one of the nuns took the veil, and for the first time the numerous visitors were excluded from the interior of the convent. This caused great dissatisfaction, and some of the sisters said, " Wait and see when M. Arnauld comes ; his daughter will not dare to keep him out." They had not long to wait. Mère Angélique wrote to her family to prepare her father for the change in the arrangements ; but either they did not dare to tell him, or he did not choose to believe them. On the twenty-fifth of September, 1609, word came to Port Royal that Monsieur and Madame Arnauld, with three of their children, the eldest brother and two sisters of the abbess, might be expected in the course of the morning.

The keys were taken from the custody of the portresses and intrusted to sisters who, by watching and prayer with Mère Angélique, had been nerved to resist the assault. While the community was at dinner, between ten and eleven o'clock, the sound of carriage-wheels was heard, and those who were in the confidence of the abbess repaired to their posts. Mère Angélique, who had been for some time at prayer in the church, hastened to the main entrance, at which her father was already knocking. She opened the wicket. M. Arnauld demanded instant admission without listening to his daughter, who entreated him to go to the parlor and hear what she had to say.

But he only knocked the louder and clamored for admittance, ending by overwhelming Mère Angélique with abuse. The mother, standing near by, added her vehement reproaches, calling her an unnatural child. The brother, just twenty-one, accused her of being nothing less than a monster and a parricide, and shouted to the nuns " to come and interfere, and not allow a man like his father, and a family like theirs, to be thus outraged and insulted." One old sister, the same who had held to her garden, responded from within, and declared that it was shameful not to open the door for M. Arnauld, while the domestics, assembled in an inner court, murmured loudly at the ingratitude of the lady abbess. M. Arnauld, meanwhile, perceiving that all this noise was useless, bethought him of a stratagem, and demanded his little daughters, Agnès and Marie-Claire, then on a visit to their sister, thinking no doubt to rush in as they opened the door. But Mère Angélique, hastily intrusting to a faithful sister the key of a little door communicating with the church, sent them out by that way. The brother continued his abuse of Mère Angélique before these little girls, but was interrupted by Agnès, who exclaimed, looking as grave and dignified as a Spanish Infanta, " My sister is only doing as she is commanded by the Council of Trent." " Listen to her," cried the brother. " Here is another one talking to us of canons and councils." During all this scene, the two sisters who had come in the carriage stood apart, sad and silent, aghast at their father's rage, and distressed by the knowledge of what Mère Angélique was suffering. M. Arnauld ordered that the horses should be instantly reharnessed to the carriage ; but on the reiterated supplications of his daughter, he consented to go first into the parlor for a moment. There he changed his tactics, and when she drew back the curtain from the grating their eyes met for the first time that day, and she saw the pale, excited face of her offended father. He spoke to her tenderly, and adjured her by the memories of the past, by their love for one another, not to treat him so ignominiously; saying at last, as he saw she remained inflexible, "Since it is all over, then, and we shall never meet again, remember my last words: Do not injure yourself, my child, by indiscreet austerities." These tender accents were too much for her to bear; she fell fainting to the floor. He tried in vain to open the grating, and called loudly for help. The nuns, not knowing what had happened, were afraid to show themselves; but the family came to the rescue, and thundered at the convent gate till they made themselves understood. All the sisters rushed to the parlor, and after some time Mère Angélique was restored to consciousness. Turning her eyes at once towards the grating, she saw her father anxiously watching her, and feebly murmured, "If he will only grant me this, not to go away to-day!" He could not refuse. The abbess was carried to her room, but she soon insisted on being brought back to a bed placed close to the grating, where she could talk to her family. The conversation became gentle and affectionate. That day and the next she reasoned with her father, and at last persuaded him to consent to his exclusion from the interior of the convent. The agreement was afterward modified so that he could give orders in regard to the buildings and the gardens; but he never again set foot in the cloister. The 25th of September, *la journée du guichet*, as it is called, was ever after celebrated in the annals of Port Royal, and after this *coup d'état* Mère Angélique had no more difficulty in carrying out the reforms she desired in her own convent. Even when she thought best to dispense with the pecuniary aid hitherto derived from her father, she was cheerfully seconded by the nuns, who had begun to regard her as a saint ; and her whole family treated her with affectionate reverence. Jeanne, now Mère Agnès, became her prioress ; Marie-Claire, as well as a remarkable younger sister, Marie Eugénie, entered the convent. In time to come we shall see her mother, also, a nun at Port Royal, as well as her sister, Madame Le Maître, who had made an unhappy marriage, and whose five sons subsequently swelled the ranks of the Solitaires.

After some years, Port Royal came to be considered as leaven for other communities, and sisters from that convent were in great demand to inaugurate reform elsewhere. Mère Angélique herself was sent to Maubuisson, where, since the death of Henry IV., disorders of all sorts were still rife, no longer shielded by the name and presence of the king. Louis XIII. himself gave the order for investigation and reform in this instance. Several ecclesiastics, sent there to report, had been shamefully maltreated, however, and the last royal commissioner had been seized with his suite, shut up in one of the towers of the abbey, and kept there for four days on bread and water, the commissioner himself receiving lashes every morning by the express command of the lady abbess herself. Such high-handed defiance could not be allowed to remain unpunished. With the consent of the Maréchal d'Estrées, her brother, and that of other members of the culprit's family, it was decided to proceed at once to extremities, and the abbot of Citeaux presented himself at Maubuisson, as though in his ordinary official capacity. Madame d'Estrées refused to appear, however, and the abbot was forced to depart without seeing her. Arrest and imprisonment were the only resource. After a long delay, the requisite order was obtained from Parliament, and the following year the abbot left Paris once more for Maubuisson, this time with a provost and archers to do his bidding. The escort was left at Pontoise, and the abbot presented himself alone at the convent-gate. During two days he tried peaceful negotiations in vain; Madame d'Estrées remained invisible, said she was ill, and laughed to scorn the threat of arrest. Finally, one morning the provost and archers were admitted at an early hour by the abbot to the outer part of the convent where he had been lodged. Under his orders, they broke open the doors, escaladed the walls, and gained access to the interior. The abbess was not to be found, however, and only at nightfall was her hiding-place discovered. She stood at bay, and made such desperate resistance that they were forced to carry her, half undressed, on a mattress to the carriage they had in waiting, and in this state she was taken to a Magdalen asylum, where orders were given that she should be kept in close confinement. Mère Angélique was appointed to the vacant place, and, accompanied by her sister Marie-Claire and two or three other nuns, she arrived at Maubuisson a fortnight after the capture of Madame d'Estrées. She found in the abbey about twenty nuns, almost all sent there against their will, and shamefully ignorant of the first rudiments of a religious education. They spent a great deal of time in preparing for dramatic entertainments that took place in the presence of large companies of invited guests. There were all kinds of amusements besides. Summer days, after hurrying through vespers and complines, the prioress took the nuns to row on the ponds near the highway to Paris, and the monks of Saint Martin de Pontoise, near by, often came of an evening to dance with the sisters. Mère Angélique and her nuns must have seemed to these people like beings of another world. She tried at first to win the old inmates, whom she had known during the two years she passed at Maubuisson, and after a time a certain amount of decency and outward conformity was secured; but to create a different atmosphere, she made the experiment of receiving at once into the convent thirty young girls, with whom she labored night and day more hopefully and not in vain, as it proved. All at once Madame d'Estrées escaped from durance vile and burst upon them at the abbey. The following account is from the lips of Mère Angélique, taken down by her nephew, M. Le Maître.

"In the month of September, 1619, Madame d'Estrées appeared unexpectedly at Maubuisson, accompanied by the Comte de Sanzai and several gentlemen. She obtained access to the convent by means of a false key, procured for her by one of the sisters, a worthless person. As we were entering the choir she approached me, and said: 'I have come, madame, to thank you for the care you have taken of my convent, and to beg you to return at once to your own, and to leave Maubuisson to me.' I answered, 'Madame, I would certainly do so if I could; but I am not here, as you know, by my own will, but by that of the abbot of Citeaux, our superior. I came by his order, and I can only go away at his command.' She replied that she was the abbess, and that she intended to take her rightful place. I said, 'Madame, you are no longer the abbess, since you have been deposed.' She answered, 'I have appealed from that decision.' I said, 'The decree holds good, as the sentence of deposition has not been annulled; and I must consider you as deposed, since I am established in this house by the abbot of Citeaux, with the authority of the king; therefore, do not take it ill that I seat myself in the abbess' place,' and thereupon I sat down. Supported by the newly received sisters, I then addressed the community, and recommended them to partake of the sacrament during mass, and to invoke the Divine aid in the storm that was impending. Most of them were already prepared for the communion, since it was a festival of our Order. I felt sure that she would turn me out; but great was my astonishment after dinner, when the confessor came to tell me that I must retire and yield to force. I answered that I should not do so, that it was against my conscience. But I was still more surprised later, when I saw him enter the church in company with Madame d'Estrées, the Comte de Sanzai, and four gentlemen with their swords drawn, and exhort me to yield, to avert the consequences of resistance. One of the gentlemen presently fired off a pistol, thinking doubtless to terrify me. But I answered, composedly, that I would not leave, unless forcibly compelled to do so; for only thus could I be excused in the sight of God. My nuns all crowded round me, putting their hands in my girdle, so that I could hardly breathe. Madame d'Estrées became very angry and abusive, and reaching out her hand, she touched or pulled my veil a little, as if she would pull it from my head. Whereupon the sisters changed from lambs to lions, not suffering that I should be harmed. One of them, Anne de Sainte-Thècle, a tall girl of noble birth, took a step towards Madame d'Estrées, and said, 'Wretched creature! are you so bold as to touch the veil of madame of Port Royal? I know you well; I know what you are!' and so saying, in presence of these men with drawn swords, she snatched the veil off her head and threw it far from her. Then Madame d'Estrées, seeing me resolved not to go, ordered the gentlemen to take me out by force, which they did, holding me by the arms. I did not resist, for I was glad to go away with my nuns from a place where there were such men, from whom I had everything to fear for the nuns and for me. But it did not suit Madame d'Estrées that they should go too, and she called to the gentlemen to put me all alone in a coach that was in waiting. As soon as I was seated, however, nine or ten of the nuns jumped in, three mounted on the box beside the coachman, and three got up behind like footmen; the rest all clung to the wheels. Madame d'Estrées ordered the coachman to whip up his horses; but he answered that he dared not do it for fear of killing some of the nuns. Then I threw myself out of the coach, and was followed by all the sisters. I bade them get some cordials, because the pestilence was at Pontoise, whither we went, the thirty nuns walking two and two in procession along the road. The lieutenant of Pontoise, a friend of Madame d'Estrées, passed on horseback, and laughed to see us. No doubt the poor man thought she was safely re-established. The people of Pontoise came out to receive us with blessings, saying, as we passed, 'There are the good nuns of the abbess of Port Royal. They have left the devil behind at Maubuisson.' We entered the first church on our way. It was the Jesuits', and they came forward to greet us very courteously; but after we had said our prayers, we left, and outside I met M. Du Val of the Sorbonne, whom I knew very well. He said that all the religious houses of Pontoise would be open to receive us; but I preferred to go somewhere by ourselves, and the prior offered me his own house, which I accepted. Meantime, an express had been sent to Paris to alarm the family. My father was away, but my brother made complaint and obtained an order for the arrest of Madame d'Estrées, who, with the Comte de Sanzai, fled so precipitately on the approach of the military, that she left her casket behind her. The soldiers went on to Pontoise, and brought us back at ten o'clock at night, in procession, as we went, escorted by a troop of one hundred and fifty archers on horseback, each bearing a lighted torch in his hand."

For some time it was necessary to keep a mounted patrol, day and night, at the abbey, to guard against surprise. Louis XIII. finally appointed as abbess Madame de Soissons, sister of the Duchess de Longueville, hoping that her high rank would put an end to the plots of the friends of Madame d'Estrées. Mère Angélique was requested by the king to remain, however, at Maubuisson, till the Pope's bull should arrive, confirming the appointment of Madame de Soissons. The double rule was not a success. Mère Angélique was thought too austere, and there was much dissatisfaction expressed that she had burdened the convent with her thirty new nuns, many without portions, and some of humble birth. Before going back to Port Royal, she wrote to ask if the community would consent to share their poverty with these thirty women, who had proved so faithful. A glad answer came promptly, signed by all the nuns, declaring that so far from regarding their coming as a burden, they should consider it a benediction. The income of Port Royal was twelve hundred dollars a year, one-fifth that of Maubuisson. Mère Angélique sent the letter to the general of the Order, obtained his approval, and then wrote to her mother, asking her to send coaches enough to transport the thirty nuns from Maubuisson to Port Royal. They were sent at once, with an attendant for each carriage. Mère Angélique accompanied them only as far as Paris, where it was necessary for her to remain a few days. Before taking leave of the sisters, she charged them, as soon as they caught sight of the hills that shut in the valley, and espied the steeple of the church above the tops of the trees, to repeat all together, "Set a watch, O Lord, before my mouth; keep the door of my lips," and from that moment to keep silence, till she herself should arrive and let loose their tongues. "This was done," says the chronicler, "lest the excitement and disturbance of their arrival should be an occasion of much idle talk and great waste of time." But as it was necessary that they should be known apart, she told each one to pin on her sleeve her name, written on a piece of paper. On the arrival of these timid mutes, who felt, as Racine says, as if they were bringing starvation to Port Royal, Mère Agnès and all the sisters came forth to meet them, singing the Te Deum. Like a quantity of wood thrown on a blazing fire, this large accession of numbers, far from depressing, increased the fervor of the community.

While at Maubuisson, Mère Angélique made the acquaintance and enjoyed the friendship of Saint Francis de Sales, and through him knew Madame de Chantal, with whom she became intimate. He went first to Maubuisson, at her request, to confirm one of that neglected sisterhood, then returned several times, once staying nine days. Mère Angélique sent him to Port Royal to see her sister, Mère Agnès. He was enchanted with the spot. "Truly a port-royal," he writes, and he ever after spoke of the place as "his dear delight." All the Arnauld family shared his friendship. Mère Agnès always wore on her person one of his precious letters to Madame Le Maître, who made at his knees a vow of perpetual chastity, before her husband's death allowed her to take the veil. The youngest son, afterwards the great doctor, received his blessing, and the eldest, M. d'Andilly, followed him about like his shadow.

Mère Angélique, feeling that "God was visibly with this man," begged him to be her spiritual director, and complained that hitherto she had been obliged to seek counsel here and there, as seemed best at the time. "Like a bee gathering honey from different flowers," added Saint Francis. "A comparison," says Sainte-Beuve, "savoring less of Calvary than of Hymettus." He rallied her also on her passion for austerities, of which he disapproved, and tried to convince her that it was unreasonable to expect the best service from a human being, any more than from a dumb animal, when they were deprived of proper rest and food. He writes: "Dearly beloved daughter, sleep well. By degrees, you may restrict yourself, since you wish to do so, to six hours; but believe me, to eat little, to labor hard, to have great anxieties, and to deprive the body of sleep, is to drive a tired, unfed horse to death." He said that her great activity of mind ran away with her, and that she was in too much of a hurry to attain spiritual perfection. "Why not," he continues, "catch small fish oftener, instead of such large ones once in a while?" and he reminds her that the finest trees are of the slowest growth. At that time he was certainly in sympathy with Port Royal, of which Saint-Cyran had not yet taken possession. Later, Sainte-Beuve thinks, he would have disapproved with Fénelon.

After her return from Maubuisson, Mère Angélique received a letter approving her action in taking the thirty sisters to Port Royal. It came from a remarkable man, who made the community his stronghold, stamping it ineffaceably as Jansenist, Augustinian, or, as he would have said, as Christian. This man was Jean du Vergier de Hauranne, Abbé de Saint-Cyran. Of a good family of Bayonne, he studied first at a Jesuit college, and was then sent to Louvain at the same time with the celebrated Jansenius. They met afterwards in Paris, both eagerly seeking the pure Christian doctrine, and determined to go back to the earliest authorities in their search for truth. De Hauranne, recalled to Bayonne on his father's death, carried his friend home with him, and there at Champré, an estate on the seashore, near Bayonne, belonging to the family, they remained five years absorbed in the study of the Scriptures and the Fathers, especially Saint Augustine. In after years, Saint-Cyran liked to show his friends a large old arm-chair with a desk attached. In it Jansenius studied, one may say lived; for he rarely went to bed at night. No wonder that Madame de Hauranne used to say to her son, "Take care, Jean, or you will kill that good Fleming, making him study so hard." All their exercise at Champré consisted in games of "battledoor and shuttlecock," in which they became fabulously adroit. At the end of these five years, sure of what they had only surmised in the beginning, that the church had lapsed into Pelagianism, they espoused the cause of God and Saint Augustine, declaring that if man can save himself, the logical inference must be that the intervention of the Redeemer becomes unnecessary, and that thus to exalt the Father at the expense of the Son virtually does away with Jesus Christ. Their belief that man has sinned, that for this deep-seated disease there is but one Healer, is Protestant-Calvinistic doctrine; but Saint-Cyran and his disciples accepted the "Real Presence" and the sacraments, and had no idea of leaving the church, though Saint-Cyran said boldly that for six hundred years the church could hardly be said to have existed, so great had been the corruption; that the bed of the river had remained, but that the water had ceased to flow; and he stigmatized the Council of Trent as a mere political assembly. Both Jansenius and he wrote ponderous Latin folios in support of these doctrines, dividing the name of Augustine between them for the titles, Petrus Aurelius and Petrus Augustinus; but while Jansenius confined himself to the doctrine, Saint-Cyran applied it to life, and Port Royal became the nursery of his seedlings. "What is the knowledge of a truth that is never put in practice?" he used to say. The "Frequent Communion," written in French by the great Arnauld, and translations of Saint Augustine, by d'Andilly and others, helped to disseminate their teachings far and wide in France, among the laity and in religious communities.

Good men, intellectually timid, like Saint Vincent de Paul, shuddered at these bold utterances, and used all their influence in Rome and at the court of France to silence Saint-Cyran. He excited a great deal of ecclesiastical jealousy by his potent influence as a spiritual director, and in this way had incurred the enmity and secured the ill-will of the notorious Capuchin, Père Joseph. Richelieu himself was at first inclined to favor and flatter the abbé. Once passing through the antechamber, on his way to a royal audience, he said to the assembled courtiers, putting his hand on Saint-Cyran's shoulder as he spoke, "This is the most learned man in Europe." But the abbé's persistent refusal of bishoprics, his criticism of the decree annulling the marriage of the king's brother, and his intimacy with Jansenius, who had just published "Mars Gallicus," a Latin pamphlet opposing Richelieu's policy, showed that he could not be won over, and caused him to be regarded by the great minister with suspicion and dislike. Finally, his conversion of M. Le Maître, the eminent lawyer and brilliant orator, who at once disappeared from the world, attracted general attention to the wide-spreading spiritual dominion of the man, and Richelieu determined to put him out of the way. "This Basque," he said, "is more dangerous than six armies. If they had imprisoned Luther and Calvin when they began to dogmatize, it would have saved a great deal of trouble." Saint-Cyran received a domiciliary visit, his papers were seized, and he was taken to Vincennes and kept there on a vague charge of heresy a whole year before he could obtain an examination. Even then he was not set at liberty, and he was only released, two years after his incarceration, at the death of Richelieu. His health had suffered from the severity of his confinement, and he did not live very long after recovering his freedom. It was a day of silence when the joyful news came to Port Royal. Mère

Angélique could not keep it to herself, and told the nuns by untying her girdle before them. She had found at last her ideal director, a man of adamantine purity, immense enthusiasm, great tenderness, and a boundless devotion to truth, and she was guided by him to the end. Ampère calls him the Lycurgus of that Christian Sparta.

For some years there had been a Port Royal also in Paris, a large house in the Faubourg Saint Jacques, now the hospital of La Maternité, purchased with the aid and at the suggestion of Madame Arnauld, at a time when the valley seemed particularly malarious. Indeed, only in modern times has the drainage been complete and the lovely spot made salubrious. Here in Paris, young girls were educated; and the same work was carried on for boys by the Solitaires, in the deserted house of Port Royal des Champs, and in neighboring châteaux belonging to noblemen friendly to the community.

When M. Le Maître retired from the world after his conversion, he lived, at first, a life of perfect seclusion in a little house built for him adjoining the convent. His brothers and nephews joined him, also under Saint-Cyran's influence; and there gradually was formed a remarkable group of men, — physicians, men of letters, soldiers, scholars, and ecclesiastics, — resolved to lead a life of self-renunciation and consecration, and who, directed by the abbé from his prison, took for their rallying-cry, "Thought allied with faith," and made redemption of souls their mission. These men were the Solitaires. They took no vows; some came and went; but the majority remained at Port Royal des Champs, systematically dividing their time between religious exercises, literary pursuits, teaching, and manual labor. The nuns also carried on various industries, and they made themselves farmers, gardeners, carpenters, and shoemakers in the service of these sisters, whom they called "Nos dames, nos maîtresses, et nos reines." They devised a plan of religious service to alternate with the convent hours, so that prayer and praise might rise perpetually at Port Royal. Of these men the saintly princess, Madame Elizabeth, sister of Louis XVI., writes: "Their theology apart, that I do not understand, these gentlemen of Port Royal were holy persons. What a life they led, compared to ours!" Their schools, called "Les petites écoles de Port Royal," soon acquired a great reputation. Their text-books were novelties, written by the Solitaires themselves, who anticipated in many ways modern ideas in regard to education. In learning languages they believed that a great deal of translation should precede grammar, and they gave their pupils copious draughts of literature. The list of their books is very long; but we may mention the French grammar by the great Arnauld, aided by Lancelot; methods of learning Greek, Latin, Spanish, and Italian, and the "Garden of Greek Roots," in French verse, by Lancelot and De Saci. They also made translations of Phædrus, Terence, Plautus, Cicero, and Virgil. They paid less attention to Latin versification than was usual at that time; but occasionally a subject was given to the older classes on which they were to improvise conjointly a copy of Latin verses. The work was done in class; every one was at liberty to contribute phrase or epithet, to suggest, to criticise, obtaining permission to speak by raising the hand, and the observation of parliamentary rules obviated all confusion. Greek was taught in these schools for the first time without a Latin medium, a great innovation, and when the "Garden of Greek Roots" is criticised it must be remembered that there was then no such thing as a Greek and French dictionary in existence. They preferred young scholars, chosen from good but not necessarily rich or noble families. People of means paid five hundred livres a year for instruction, which was gratuitous to others. They taught children to read first in French instead of in Latin, another innovation; and Pascal suggested the method they employed of pronouncing at first only the vowel sounds of the alphabet, leaving the consonants to be learned afterwards in combination with the vowels; the base, it will be seen, of the phonetic system now generally adopted in France. For writing, they were the first to use metal pens, for the purpose, they say, of "saving the time of teachers and scholars." Saint-Cyran agreed with Erasmus that six scholars were enough for one teacher, and when they had twenty-four pupils, they placed them in four separate rooms, with a master for each. At the Château de Chesnai a whole wing was given up to the children.

The severest punishment was to be sent home, or to see some service assigned to a servant that the pupil was accustomed to perform for his teacher. Great gentleness and indulgence were required of the teachers, who were to endeavor to make study as interesting as amusement. There were out-of-door recreations and such indoor amusements as billiards, backgammon, chess, or historical games of cards. A formal politeness was enforced, every one being addressed as Monsieur. Saint-Cyran had always wished to devote himself to children, and was very fond of teaching them. Before his imprisonment, he went every other day to Port Royal, superintended the boys' work, more especially their themes, and gave them a commentary on Virgil. The largest of these schools were at the Château de Chesnai near Port Royal, and in a *cul-de-sac* of the Rue Saint Dominique in Paris. These were broken up on the charge of being nests of heresy, and the teachers were obliged to disguise and hide themselves, in constant danger of arrest and imprisonment. The Hôtel de Longueville and other great houses sheltered two or three at a time. De Saci, nephew of Mère Angélique, was thrown into the Bastille, where he passed two years, occupied in translating the Old Testament in French. He had already translated the New. Copies of his Bible, printed by the Elzevirs, and smuggled into Paris in produce-wagons, under convoy of some man of mark, were afterwards widely distributed.

When the nuns returned to Port Royal des Champs, the Solitaires betook themselves to Les Granges, a farm on the heights, less than a third of a mile from the abbey. They did not see much of the sisters, though in such close sympathy and working always in concert. Mère Angélique did not approve of very frequent visits, and the cloister rule was strictly observed. The uncle of Madame de Sévigné, a devoted friend of Port Royal, built a new cloister for the nuns, and after its completion sent to ask if he could be admitted only once, accompanying his request by the present of a basket of rare fruit. Mère Agnès answered, "I thank you humbly for the fruit. You have the privilege of giving as much as you like and of granting every favor that is asked. Both these privileges are denied us, so that you cannot see the inside of our building on account of an angel with a flaming sword at the gate, I mean the anathema of the church." The Chevalier de

Sévigné entered the promised land at last; but only after his death. He was buried in his cloister.

Another note from Mère Agnès to her nephew shows that she was more indulgent than her sister in regard to visits from the Solitaires.

To M. Le Maître:—

LES GRANGES.

My very dear Nephew,—I believe that you think I have gone back to Paris, or else that I have come here to live as if I were excommunicated, it is so long since you have asked for me; and I avail myself of the privileges of an aunt and an old woman to ask you to come to the parlor of Sainte Madeleine at noon to-day to be scolded for your conduct.

At one time Mère Angélique had been made superior of the convent of the Saint Sacrement in Paris, afterwards incorporated with Port Royal, and on this occasion, when a uniform dress was required, the sisters adopted the white scapulars of the Saint Sacrement with a large red cross in front, a very striking costume.

A new superior at Citeaux threatening to put an end to all eccentricity — meaning austerity — at Port Royal, Mère Angèlique, alarmed, petitioned for a change of jurisdiction, and obtained permission from the Pope to belong to the diocese of Paris. She had no more monkish interference to apprehend; but the archbishops of Paris were very much controlled by the court, and this influence proved, in the end, fatal to Port Royal. There had been still another important change. While Louis XIII. was besieging La Rochelle, his mother, Marie de Médicis, paid a visit to the abbey, and said to Mère Angélique, as she was going away, "Have you nothing to ask of me? the first time I go to a convent, I always grant some favor." Mère Angélique asked that the abbess should be in future elected every three years, instead of being chosen for life.

This was done, and she immediately resigned her place, together with her coadjutrix, Mère Agnès. In course of time they were both re-elected, but Mère Angélique had reason frequently to repent of her abdication.

The wars of the Fronde disturbed the industrious, peaceful seclusion of the valley. The convent was put in a state of defence, and the Solitaires manned the walls and made ready for a siege. Even M. Le Maître wore a sword by his side, or carried a musket over his shoulder. The nuns of neighboring convents flocked in to seek an asylum, and were received with open arms, as well as the poor peasants, who were allowed to store their valuables in the church itself. The convent courts were full of cattle, and the monastery looked like Noah's ark.

Port Royal had helped Cardinal Retz when, as archbishop of Paris, he was sorely in need, and he was always amiable to Mère Angélique and often friendly to the community; but no reliance could be placed upon him, and little sympathy was possible between these disciples of Saint-Cyran and that Don Juan of a prelate. As some one said, "He, a Jansenist? Impossible; to be a Jansenist, you must be a Christian."

The Jesuits incessantly defamed Port Royal, and Jansenius' book, "Petrus Augustinus," had been condemned by a bull of Urbain VIII., confirmed more definitely by his successor, Innocent X. The Syndic of the Faculty of Theology in Paris had distinguished himself, moreover, by denouncing specifically five propositions, which he said were contained in the book. From this time the enemies of Port Royal knew where to aim. The Jesuits in Rome then sent word that if some of the French clergy would ask for the condemnation of these five propositions, the

Holy Father would not be averse to granting their request. Saint Vincent de Paul eagerly headed the movement in Paris, and the petition was sent to Rome without first submitting it to the general assembly of the clergy then in session. On account of this irregularity, Innocent hesitated ; but the regent, Anne of Austria, at the suggestion of Saint Vincent de Paul, signified to the Pope her wish that he would act promptly and decisively in the matter, whereupon he signed the bull.

This caused great rejoicing in the Jesuit camp; all courtiers disclaimed the slightest Jansenistic taint, and such a horror prevailed in these circles, of the Augustinian doctrine of grace, that a story is told of an orthodox bishop, on a visit to an abbey of his diocese, who hearing, as he entered the refectory, these words pronounced by the reader : "It is God who worketh in us to will and to do," called out, "Close that book, and bring it to me at once." He was obeyed, and the heretical author was discovered to be Saint Paul!

Mazarin cared little for these theological disputes; but he owed the Jansenists a grudge and was suspicious of their amicable relations with Retz. Gondi at first resisted the king's order that the bishops should formally accept the Pope's bull, but when Anne of Austria said cajolingly that he must not refuse the first favor she had ever asked of him, the gallant courtier gave way, and that barrier was thrown down.

This was the Formulary that all priests, monks, and nuns were eventually required to sign : "I submit in good faith to the ordinances of his Holiness, Innocent X., and I condemn in my heart and by word of mouth the five propositions of Cornelius Jansenius, contained in the book entitled 'Petrus Augustinus,' which the Pope and the bishops have condemned, which doctrine is not that of Saint Augustine, but which the said Jansenius has perverted contrary to the meaning of the worthy doctor."

The Parliament of Paris was in no haste to register the decree requiring these signatures, and Mazarin declared openly that the king had already done more than he ought for the Jesuits, who gave him more trouble than all the government of the realm. In the mean time the Sorbonne called to account for his doctrines the author of the "Frequent Communion," the great Arnauld, youngest brother of Mère Angélique. He was publicly censured; but it is asserted that the Sorbonne had been packed for the vote with a large number of newly made doctors, ignorant and obsequious to the regent. While the trial was going on, she remarked one day to the Princesse de Guémené, a great friend of Port Royal, "Your doctors talk too much." — "That need not disturb you, madame," retorted the princess; "you have already on the benches more mendicant monks and friars than you need." — "And there are more to come," said the queen, haughtily. — "Do put an end to this affair!" Mazarin exclaimed one day to one of the doctors; "these women do nothing but talk about it, and they understand it no better than I do." Arnauld's defence was in Latin, and Port Royal made use of Pascal's pen to appeal from the Sorbonne to the public. Then appeared "Les Lettres Provinciales." This fierce assault, these deadly blows dealt by a skilful and unsparing hand, fairly took away the enemy's breath. The immediate success is well known: the letters became the rage, the next issue was eagerly anticipated, and choice circles gathered to hear them read aloud in the salons of the

Duchesse de Longueville, the Princesse de Conti, the Princesse de Guéméné, and Madame de Sablé. It only made it more interesting that no one knew exactly when the next letter would appear or where they were printed, and that the bookseller had made his fortune and had been thrown into the Bastille. Pascal's relations with Port Royal had attracted very little attention, and he was known principally as a mathematician and man of fashion ; but a rumor of his being the author obliged him to hide and disguise himself. He lodged at this time, under an assumed name, in a small inn near the Sorbonne, directly opposite the college of the Jesuits, — in the lion's mouth, as it were. His brother-in-law, M. Périer, from Auvergne, arriving in Paris for a few days, went to the same house, where he received one day a visit from an old acquaintance, one of the Fathers opposite. In the course of conversation the priest said, "Do you know that some people suppose that your brother, M. Pascal, is the author of these letters?" M. Périer replied as unconcernedly as he could, while he was painfully aware that behind the half-closed curtains of the bed near which they were seated, twenty or more copies of the next letter, fresh from the press, were spread out to dry. When the guest had gone, Pascal came down from his room overhead, heard the story, and took possession of his property. There was now a lull. The Solitaires, dispersed by a royal mandate, quietly swarmed again in their old haunts, the schools revived, and everything in the community was prosperous and peaceful, when the long-gathering storm broke over Port Royal. The king issued an order to disperse boarders and scholars, novices and postulants, and furthermore commanded that none should be received in future. Mère

Angélique had truly said, " Yes, we shall kill the dragon ; but he will be our death." M. Singlin, too, the superior, was also sent away. Mère Angélique hastened to Paris to aid her sister, Mère Agnès. She took leave of her nuns as if she should never see them again. She was nearly seventy years old, and very feeble. To her brother, M. d'Andilly, she said, as he was helping her into the carriage, " Keep a brave heart." — " Trust me, my sister," was his response ; " I shall not be found wanting." — " My brother, my brother," she replied, " let us be humble, and remember that humility without firmness is cowardice, but that courage without humility is presumption." In her clear vision she saw the temptation to martyrdom, and dreaded for her friends vain-glory in suffering for God almost as much as faint-heartedness. Deprived of her director, M. Singlin, and not choosing that her beloved nephew, De Saci, should expose himself to the danger of arrest by coming to the house on her account, she said to the sisters who expressed their sorrow for her deprivation, " It does not trouble me ; I know that M. Singlin is praying for me. What more could I ask ? I respect him very much ; but I do not put a man in the place of God. My nephew without God's help could do me no good, and God without him shall be all in all." They walled up the doors, shutting them out from their own gardens ; and when some of the sisters said, " Who knows but that they may be shutting themselves out of heaven ? " she reproved them, saying, " Do not speak so, my daughters, but pray to God for them and for us." After a few days her feebleness increased, dropsical symptoms appeared, and she was confined to her bed. Troubled by the idea that the nuns would keep a record of her last words and actions as if she were a saint, she tried to speak very little, and to do nothing that could excite remark. She knew that they had already done so to some extent, and she had a horror of the twaddle in the " Lives of the Saints," and of sentimental death-bed recitals. She summoned all her energy to write a letter to the queen-mother, pleading the cause of Port Royal, defending the community from the charge of heresy, and invoking in their favor the testimony of Saint Francis de Sales and Madame Chantal. She quoted from Saint Thérèse to remind her majesty that in a court it is not always an easy matter to ascertain the truth. This duty accomplished, she laid herself down to die, saying, "It is time for a little sabbath rest." Strange to say, only towards the last was this admirable woman freed from an overpowering dread. Of this terror her brother writes: "May it not show an ardent imagination, an unusually powerful conception of the holiness and justice of the Supreme Being, denoting a great soul?"

The history of Port Royal has sometimes been called nothing but a quarrel between the Jesuits and the Arnauld family. As we stand by the open grave of their acknowledged head, let us pass them in review as if they gathered from far and near from the spirit-land to do her reverence.

Antoine Arnauld, father of Mère Angélique, had twenty children, ten of whom lived to grow up. His wife took the veil after her husband's death, and passed the last twelve years of her life in the Paris convent. The eldest son, M. Arnauld d'Andilly, who was the first to feel Saint-Cyran's influence, was a genial person, more receptive than original, very susceptible to female charms, courtly and amiable, but upright and loyal withal, — like seaweed, waving about on the water, but firmly fastened to the rock beneath. He was more literary than any other of the family, and did Port Royal good service by his finished translations from Saint Augustine, his constant oversight and criticism, and his knowledge of the world. He refused a place offered him in the Academy; and upon this occasion Richelieu made the rule, ever since strictly observed, that no places should ever be offered, and that candidates for the honor should make personal application. M. d'Andilly lived to a great age and served to the last as an usher, — a sort of self-appointed master of ceremonies for the nuns in their dark days, a connecting-link between Port Royal and the world without. He was one of the Solitaires, built himself a house on the hill near Les Granges, and spent his own fortune and part of his eldest son's also in draining and embellishing the grounds of the convent. His especial delight was in raising fine fruit, of which he presented propitiatory offerings to the queen-mother, Madame de Sablé, and Mademoiselle Montpensier. "La grande Mademoiselle" gives an amusing and characteristic account of a visit she paid him in "his dear desert." He had sent her a basket of cling-stone peaches, with an injunction not to eat them till they were "dead-ripe." The fruit, by the way, was not meant for the consumption of the community, but was usually sold and the proceeds given to the poor.

When the final dispersion came of the House in Paris, M. d'Andilly was on the spot, affording his protection to the sisters, escorting the nuns to their carriages, and, when his daughters' turn came, first leading them into the church before the altar as if to consecrate them anew in the cause of truth and to the service of God. Constant as he was to his outlawed belief, and courageous in his devotion to his persecuted family and friends, he never appears to have forfeited the royal favor; and the queen-mother could ask, even while urging on the enemies of Port Royal, "Does d'Andilly love me still?" He was also a great favorite at the Hôtel Rambouillet, and in his youth belonged to that set. He had two daughters, Mère Angélique Saint-Jean and Sister Madeline Thérèse, both nuns at Port Royal. Of the eldest her father said to Madame de Sévigné, "Depend upon it, I myself and all my other children are stupid in comparison with Angélique." On her, indeed, the mantle of her aunt seemed to fall. M. d'Andilly had six sisters, who were all nuns: Madame Le Maître, Mère Angélique, Mère Agnès, Sister Anne Eugénie, Sister Marie-Claire, and Sister Madeleine Sainte Christine. Of his three brothers, the eldest was the Bishop of Angers, and the second, Simon, a young soldier, was killed at Verdun. The youngest became celebrated as "the Great Arnauld," eulogized by Voltaire, and for whom Boileau wrote the epitaph beginning : —

"Errant, pauvre, banni, proscrit, persecuté."

Madame Le Maître had five sons, all Solitaires : M. Le Maître, the eminent orator, and MM. de Saci, Séricourt, Saint-Elme, and Valemont. The name Saci is thought to be an anagram of Isaac.

Mère Angélique was sometimes considered too austere. She was certainly less indulgent than Mère Agnès, and had little patience with the wearisome caprices of some of their fine-lady converts; but no real grief, even of a crowned head, appealed to her in vain. Marie de Gonzagne, beloved of Cinq-Mars, afterwards Queen of Poland, had a lodging at Port Royal des Champs, and she appeared as a mourner at Saint-Cyran's funeral. After her departure for Poland, she kept up a constant correspondence with Mère Angélique, and offered the community a refuge from persecution in her kingdom when she learned that they were seriously thinking of embarking for America. When we read the description of Mère Angélique's tenderness to Jacqueline Pascal at the time of her taking the veil, we are reminded of what the sisters used to say of her: "If she is as terrible as an angel, she can comfort you like one."

The community was accused by its enemies of the heinous sin of not worshipping saints, and of caring little for images; and we might think Port Royal free from superstition, were it not for the famous story of the cure of Pascal's little niece by the application of a reliquary containing one of the sacred thorns from the crown worn by Jesus, to a tumor of the lachrymal gland. The cure was said to have been immediate and miraculous. Pascal himself was profoundly impressed, never seeming for a moment to doubt the authenticity of the miracle; and Mère Angélique gives Marie de Gonzague a detailed account of the cure, appearing to believe in it devoutly. Then a daughter of Philippe de Champagne was cured at Port Royal of a chronic disease, in answer, it was said, to the prayers of the community, — an event commemorated by her father in a picture in the Louvre representing Mère Agnès and his daughter. Long after the destruction of Port Royal this idea of miracle-working revived among the so-called Jansenists, and reached its climax in the extravagances of the "Convulsionnaires of Saint Médard."

At the time of the departure of Mère Angélique for

Paris, Jacqueline Pascal had been left in charge of Port Royal des Champs, and upon her devolved the responsibility of accepting or rejecting the Formulary when it was presented for signature. The decision was made even harder on account of a preamble written by Pascal himself, at the request of some of the clergy, who did not object to leaving a loophole for the consciences of the sisterhood. But the anguish of these women was great. If the preamble was obscure, the Formulary was clear. How could they condemn the doctrine of Jansenius in which they believed, or assert that the Five Propositions were in a book that they had never read, and which they could not read? Jacqueline Pascal writes in a letter, indorsed, "To be shown to my brother if he is well enough:" "I know the respect I owe the bishops, but my conscience will not let me sign a statement that a thing is in a place where I have never seen it. . . . How can they cut us off from the church? They can deprive us of the outward signs of that union, but never of the union itself so long as we have love one for another. . . . How is this that we are asked to do different from offering incense to idols, and thinking that we are absolved because we have a piece of the cross hidden in our sleeves?" (an allusion to a passage in one of the "Lettres Provinciales"); and farther on, "I know that it is not for women to defend the faith, but when bishops are as timorous as women, it befits women to be as brave as bishops." Jacqueline's rebuke sank into her brother's heart. From that time he rejected all subterfuges and compromises; and when his sister died, not long afterwards, he only said to those who brought the tidings, "God grant that our end may be like hers!"

When it was urged upon Mère Angélique-Saint-Jean that she should sign the Formulary as an act of submission, to avoid scandal, she replied: "To me it seems as if a surgeon had bandaged my arm for no cause whatever, and when it had become inflamed and swollen, proposed to cut it off to avoid gangrene. Should I not be justified in saying to him, 'Cut off your bandage, but do not cut off my arm'?" When threatened with the papal anathema, she said: "There is one consolation: the successors of Saint Peter are very apt to imitate his haste in drawing the sword, and they strike without awaiting their Master's command. Then Jesus comes and heals the wound."

These women were no respecters of persons, and it is not hard to understand how offensive their practical, uncompromising republicanism must have been to the court hard by, at Versailles. So long as they did not bow down, Louis XIV. felt as if he did not really reign. They stood steadfast, gently inflexible, bearing in mind how Mère Angélique had said, "I fear nothing that is not eternal," refusing to compound with their consciences in spite of the persuasions and entreaties of their friends, and the threatening taunts of their enemies, who wielded against them, defenceless as they were, the combined power of the king and pope. "Pure as angels, and proud as demons," said the archbishop of Paris.

When the king was told of their determined disobedience, he resolved that the punishment should be condign. The nuns were forcibly removed and imprisoned separately, or two or three together, in different convents. Some gave way, but most remained firm. After a long time the unrepentant sisters who still remained alive were sent back to Port Royal, where they remained imprisoned three or four years under an interdict, deprived of the sacraments, and with sentinels posted night and day outside their walls. At last, under a new Pope, the "Peace of the Church" was proclaimed, the stubborn bishops were pardoned, and Louis XIV., in good humor after his Peace of Aix-la-Chapelle, declared that he would not be "more severe with the nuns than the Pope had been with the clergy." The moment was thought propitious, the sisters made a tardy and vague submission, and the interdict was removed. Great was the rejoicing in the valley when the long-silent bells rang out again. The Great Arnauld, who had just been presented at court, said the first high mass at Port Poyal, and was still at the altar, when a long procession with banners and music from the parish of Magny, near by, entered the church to join in their thanksgiving services.

Ten years of prosperity ensued; but immediately after the death of the Duchesse de Longueville, their protectress, persecution, long smouldering, broke out afresh, and in spite of their previous submission, there was a second blockade and interdict of thirty years, ending in the forcible removal of the twenty-two surviving nuns, the youngest fifty and the eldest eighty years old. All that was asked of them was to allow a notice to be posted at the convent gate, stating that they accepted the bull of Innocent X., and submitted in all things to the papal authority; but they refused, accepted the consequences, and went down with their flag flying. They were separated and scattered in different convents, where they remained, deprived of the sacraments even in their last hours. The church, convent, outbuildings, and adjacent houses were razed to their foundations, and all the dead removed from the cemetery, by express order of the king. The desecration of the graves was frightful, and identification was intentionally rendered impossible. At this time Racine's remains were removed by his friends to St. Étienne du Mont, in Paris. His aunt had been one of the last abbesses of Port Royal. During the last ten years, these secluded women had probably excited envy as well as dislike; for they had been courted by the world of fashion to some extent, as well as esteemed by many thoughtful people who did not accept their doctrine. Ladies of high rank were in the habit of going to Port Royal for short religious retreats, and the services on holy-days seemed very attractive, fourteen or fifteen ecclesiastics often being present uninvited. Not that there was any splendor of ritual, or luxury of altar-cloth or vestments: the pictures of Philippe de Champagne were the only ornaments of the church, there was no organ, and the reading and singing, though beautiful, were of the simplest kind; but the fervor of the nuns and the quiet of the place constituted a peculiar charm.

The description of Port Royal in the sixth volume of the "Clélie" of Mademoiselle Scudéry, is purely imaginary: but we find this account by a M. Lonail, written in 1693:—

"It is not a large monastery, but lodges a goodly number. The court is narrow and long, extending from east to west. The church, the parlors, and the houses of female guests are on one side, and the stables, workshops, and houses for ecclesiastics and male guests on the other. The cloister and dwellings of the nuns are apart, behind the church. The garden extends towards the east, and is intersected by a little canal. Towards the south there is a shady wood by a brook, called the Solitude. All this is shut in by high walls, defended at intervals by towers, built during the wars of the Fronde to protect the convent from soldiery." After describing the church, the cloisters, and the procession, he continues: "At last I left a place where I would willingly have stayed all my life. I climbed the hill to the left and visited Les Granges, the farm of the Solitaires. There I saw the old schools of Port Royal, the houses of M. d'Andilly and M. Arnauld, and the Solitude of M. Pont-Château. I turned back to look once more on the abbey and the fields tilled by these pious men, and bade adieu to this blessed spot; but the memory of my visit lingers like a perpetual feast."

The destruction has been complete. All that remains of the abbey of Port Royal is the dove-cote, a large round tower, with a funnel-shaped roof; fragments of pillars and capitals; the Fountain of Mère Angélique; a large walnut-tree, that goes by her name; Les Granges on the neighboring heights; and the walk called La Solitude, with its rusty, ivy-garlanded cross. The church was a fine specimen of the Cistercian architecture in the early part of the thirteenth century. A little chapel has been erected on the spot where the high altar stood, and here can be seen some interesting relics, such as portraits, engravings, and manuscript letters. Some of the tombstones, rescued from desecration, are preserved in the neighboring church of Magny, Arnauld d'Andilly's among the number. You can wander about Port Royal at your will, perfectly undisturbed by guides or tourists, pace the Alley of the Solitaires by the side of the brook, that has learned not to murmur, and keeps in summer days their vow of silence, or throw yourself on the daisied grass by the old fountain or in the shade of the walnut-tree of Mère Angélique. If you wish to examine the relics, you summon the guardian in the employ of the Society of Saint Antoine, to whom the property now belongs. He is a gentle old man, upwards of eighty, a schoolmaster at Asnières for more than forty years, proud and appreciative of the treasures intrusted to his keeping, and quite imbued with the spirit of the place. After speaking of his past life and his age, he added: "I am perfectly happy. I am not afraid to die; but I sometimes think that heaven itself cannot be more peaceful than Port Royal."

From Versailles, the distance to the abbey is about eight miles, but a pleasant excursion can be made from Paris by taking the Chemin de fer de la Bretagne at the Gare Mont Parnasse early enough to connect with the little *patache* that goes from La Verrière, the second station beyond Saint-Cyr, to Mesnil-Saint-Denis. From this hamlet you go on foot. The road winds through fields for a mile and a half, skirts a wood, and the top of the "Colombier" of Port Royal soon comes in sight. The entrance is by a little door in an old stone wall. You can return another way by Trappes, a station nearer to Paris than La Verrière, but the walk is not nearly so pleasant as from Mesnil-Saint-Denis. You pass, however, by Les Granges, the farm of the Solitaires.

People say sometimes, "There is not much to see at Port Royal." That is true; but the place is redolent of beautiful memories and interesting associations, and the peace has not passed away.

THE SONG OF ROLAND

Go to the MS. department of the Bodleian Library at Oxford, and ask for "Digby 23." You will be intrusted with a little volume, worn and old, such as the "jongleur" used to take out of his pocket after he had tuned his viol at the gate of some walled town or lofty turreted castle at the end of his day's journey. This MS. is the oldest copy of an older version of a still older poem; for you hold in your hand the work of an Anglo-Norman scribe of the twelfth century, the most authentic copy of the earliest and most beautiful of the French "chansons de gestes," the first of Christian epics, the "Song of Roland."

The last line of the poem reads thus: "Here Théroulde finishes his work;" and it has been said that a tutor of William the Conqueror bore this name, that a descendant of his was Abbot of Peterborough, that the tutor was the poet, and that the abbot had this copy of the poem made for the library of his monastery. All this is surmise, however. "Théroulde déclinet" may mean only the copyist; but it is tolerably certain that this version of the epic, dating from the eleventh century, was made up in part of shorter poems on the same subject, much older, and probably lyrical, such as Charlemagne collected, and the French women used to sing to the music of the clapping of their hands. The jongleur's violin was often made of iron or copper, and sometimes he used his sword for a bow. So may have done Taillefer, the minstrel, when, as Wace relates, he led the van of the Norman army at the battle of Hastings, singing this very song "of Charlemagne, and of Roland, and of Oliver, and the nobles, who fell at Roncesvaux." Thus "to the sound of the 'Song of Roland' England was conquered by the Normans." We read how the Saxons spent the night before the battle in wassail and revelry, while the Normans went to confession and prayed as they kept watch and ward. And this song, which inspired them on the morrow, is imbued with the glow of the dawn of feudal Christianity. These rude soldiers who, says Motley, "about this time seated themselves with gentlemanlike effrontery on every throne in Europe," were comparatively recent converts, and felt like real children of the Church. Children they certainly were in their undoubting faith and imperfect comprehension of what the new religion meant; but we must not forget that they were still thrilled by the narrow escape of Christianity from destruction at the battle of Tours, "where the horsemen of the East met the footmen of the West, and three hundred thousand Arab corpses marked the point at which the flood-tide turned." So to them every foe was a Saracen, and every infidel a deadly foe. Can we wonder?

When Charlemagne, leaning against the window of his palace by the sea, watched the white sails of the Norse rovers, and wept to think of their ravages after his death, he did not dream that descendants of these very Vikings would embalm his memory in legendary lore, and hand down his name in imperishable song through ten centuries. But so it is. Thus opens the "Song of Roland:" —

> Charles the King, our great Emperor,
> Seven long years has tarried in Spain.
> Down to the sea the haughty land is his.
> Castles and towns with their embattled walls
> Lay low before him. All save one subdued,
> And that one Saragossa, on the height.
> Marsile holds sway there, and he loves not God,
> Adores Apollo, and invokes Mahmoud:
> He can not prosper.

This confusion of Pagan and Mohammedan beliefs is not uncommon in the literature of the Middle Ages. Farther on, thus Charles receives the Saracen embassy: —

> In a large orchard sits the Emperor,
> He has beside him Roland, Oliver,
> The great Duke Samson, and Anselm the proud,
> His standard-bearer, Geoffrey of Anjou,
> Gérin and Gérier, and many more.
> Full fifteen thousand gentlemen are there,
> Who come from France, "sweet France."
> . . . .
> White silken stuffs are spread
> Upon the grass. The elders and the grave
> Are playing chess, and some at "trictrac," while
> The agile youths are fencing. At his ease
> Beneath a pine, beside an eglantine,
> In a great arm-chair, all of solid gold,
> Sits Charles the King, who holds sweet France in fee.
> His beard is white, and snowy white his hair.
> So fair his features, and so proud his mien,
> No one need ask, "Which is the Emperor?"

The following passage is as remarkable in its way as the first quotation: —

> The mighty Charlemagne, by dint of blows,
> For seven long years had kept his hold on Spain.
> He captured castles and he captured towns.

THE SONG OF ROLAND 47

> The King Marsile grew anxious, and he sent,
> The first year of his stay, to Balingant.
> He was the admiral, the old Emir,
> Who lived in Babylon in Egypt. He
> Had survived Homer and Virgil. Him
> Marsile had asked for help for Saragossa.
> If 'twas refused, Marsile would leave his gods
> And all his idols for the Christian faith,
> To make his peace with Charles.

The argument of the poem is briefly this: Marsile, a Spanish king, threatened in his great stronghold Saragossa, sends messengers to Charlemagne to sue for peace. The Emperor, advised by Roland, charges Ganelon to convey his answer to the Saracen. Ganelon, angry with Roland for having suggested that he should go on such a perilous errand, secretly plots his destruction. He returns from his embassy laden with rich gifts, the price of his treason, and announces to Charles the entire submission of Marsile, who even promises to be baptized as a Christian. He thus succeeds in persuading the Emperor to recross the Pyrenees, leaving to Roland the command of the rearguard, which consists of only 20,000 men. Charlemagne, in spite of dreams and gloomy presentiments, yields, and goes back to France.

Meanwhile Marsile summons his twelve peers, gathers a large army, and comes up with the rear-guard in the Pyrenean pass of Roncesvaux, when he is quite sure that the Emperor is far away. Oliver, Roland's beloved friend and compeer, is the first to discover that they are pursued. Three times he entreats Roland to sound his horn, the famous "olifant," to call Charles to the rescue; but Roland obstinately refuses. In this part of the poem may be remarked the repetitions, or "similar stanzas," about which so much has been said; some critics urging that they are parallel accounts of the same event, fragments hitched together, while others think that it is meant to deepen the impression of the incident. Similar cases will occur to students of still older literatures. The result may be tiresome, but, as an eminent professor once observed, when it was proposed to him to cull only choice passages from this very " Song of Roland:" "You must have the tediousness, or you will not get a true idea of the poem."

> 'Tis morning. Oliver ascends a hill,
> Looks to his right across the grassy vale,
> And sees approaching all the heathen host.
> He calls aloud: "Now, Roland, what is this?
> What means yon clamor borne to us from Spain,
> These snowy hauberks and these glist'ning helms?
> Our men will be astounded at the sight.
> It is Ganilo's work, the traitor, wretch:
> Through him King Charles has brought us to this pass."
> But Roland answered: "Silence, Oliver;
> He is my step-father; no more of this."

> High is the hill where Oliver has climbed;
> Afar he looks upon the land of Spain,
> And sees the army of the Saracens,
> Their shining helmets gilt and decked with gems,
> Their bucklers, and embroidered coats of mail,
> With spears and gonfanons at lance's point.
> Innumerable squadrons crowd the plains.
> He cannot count them, and he hurries down,
> Hies to the French, and tells what he has seen.

> "Look you," says Oliver, "the Saracens
> Are swarming yonder in a countless host;
> A hundred thousand heathen with their shields.
> Laced are their helmets, and their hauberks white,
> Upright their lances, gleaming their brown spears.

French gentlemen, God give you of His strength!
You shall have battle: such there never was.
Stand well your ground, or we shall lose the day."
The Frenchmen answered: " Cursed be he who flees!
Not one of us will fail you for that death."

Then urges Oliver: "The heathen host
By far outnumbers us. Friend, sound your horn.
When Charles shall hear it, they will all come back,
The king and all his barons, to our help."
" Far be it from me," Roland answered him,
" For I should lose my glory in sweet France.
No. I will strike great blows with Durandal:
The blade shall be all ruddy to the hilt.
The wretched pagans in an evil hour
Came to these defiles: they are doomed to die."

" I pray you, Roland, sound your olifant,
For Charles on hearing it will straightway come,
He and his nobles, to our rescue." " No.
Now God forbid I bring my friends to shame,
Or sweet France to dishonor!" Roland said.
" But I will strike great blows with Durandal,
The good sword I have girded to my side:
The blade shall be all ruddy to the hilt.
The miscreant pagans in an evil hour
Have gathered here: they are condemned to die."

" I pray you, Roland, sound your olifant,
And Charles shall hear it when he's far away,
And come with all his army to our help."
" I will not do it. Not a man who lives
Shall say I wound my horn for heathen folk.
Far be it from me to disgrace my friends.
No. Where the battle rages I shall strike
Great blows with Durandal — a thousand blows,
Then seven hundred more, with that good sword
The Emperor once girded to my side:
The blade shall be all ruddy to the hilt.
The French fight well, of that I warrant you.
The pagan dogs are doomed to die the death."

> "'Tis no dishonor," Oliver replies.
> "I tell you I have seen the Saracens.
> They throng the mountains and they throng the vales;
> The plains and moorlands are all hid by them.
> Great are the numbers of this foreign host,
> And small our company." Then Roland said:
> "So much the better! I would have it so.
> I thirst for battle; and I pray to God
> And all His angels that the land of France
> May never through my means know loss or shame.
> Death rather than dishonor! Deal hard blows:
> We shall be dearer to the Emperor."

This poem was evidently written before the Crusades, but its animating spirit of hatred of the heathen and love of the Church was precisely what made the Crusades possible. Is there not a foretaste of Peter the Hermit in the benediction given by the soldier-prelate, Archbishop Turpin, to the French army, just before the fight?

> Yonder is Turpin, the Archbishop.
> Up to the brow of an o'erhanging hill
> He spurs his horse, and calls out to the French:
> "Sir Knights, our Emperor has left us here.
> We'll do our duty, though we lose our lives.
> Help in the cause of Christ, as need there be,
> You shall have battle. There you see the foe,
> The hated heathen. Now confess your sins;
> I will absolve you. Then, if you must die,
> You die as martyrs, and the highest seats
> In heaven are yours." The Frenchmen all alight,
> And kneel to take the blessing. They are told
> Their only penance is to deal hard blows.
> So says the good Archbishop.

> The miscreant pagans fiercely ride amain.
> "Look you now, Roland," shouted Oliver,
> "They are upon us, and our liege lord Charles
> Is far away. Oh! had you blown your horn,
> Charles had been here; the day would not be lost.

Cast your eyes upward toward the gates of Spain:
You see a mournful rear-guard. Men stand there
Who look their last upon a battle-field."
And Roland answered: "Shame upon such words!
Accursed be he who bears a coward heart!
Here shall we stand our ground. Ours the good blows.
We shall be victors."

Thus Roland exhorts his men before the battle: —

When Roland sees the battle close at hand,
Lion nor leopard ne'er more terrible.
He cheers his men, and says to Oliver:
"Sir Knight, companion, friend, you greatly err.
The Emperor Charles, who trusts them to our care,
Has set aside these twenty thousand men,
Chosen by him, and well he knows them brave.
For him we'll suffer, and, if need there be,
Lay down our lives."

Great is the battle, marvellous the fight.
The French deal heavy blows with their good swords:
They all are ruddy to the jewelled hilt.
"Montjoie!" they shout, the Emperor's battle-cry.
O'er all the field they press the Saracens.
The pagans see theirs is no easy task.
Great is the battle, it is horrible —
A scene of mortal anguish; men lie there
By thousands, bleeding, wounded, dying, dead,
Piled one upon another. On their backs,
Or faces downward, lie the Saracens.
Who does not flee cannot escape from death.

Roland at last, faint from his wounds, and feeling that they are in danger of being overpowered, proposes to blow his horn; but Oliver tells him it is useless, and upbraids him with not having done so before. The Archbishop rides up, reconciles them, and represents to Oliver that even now the Emperor may arrive in time to give them Christian burial. So Roland puts the "olifant" to his lips, and blows a blast that is heard ninety miles away. (The blast, tradition avers, is still resounding and re-echoing in those Pyrenean gorges.) Charles hears it. Ganelon is discovered to be a traitor, is chained up like a bear, and given in custody to the King's scullions to be beaten with rods while awaiting his trial. The French hurry back, hoping to be in time to rescue Roland.

> How high the mountains and the beetling crags!
> How deep the gorges, and how swift the streams!
> Loud blow the trumpets of the Emperor:
> Before, behind, the army loud they blow,
> And answer Roland's horn.
>
> The Emperor rides on in bitter wrath.
> The French are furious with agony:
> Not one who is not sobbing as he rides;
> Not one who is not praying God to save
> Roland in mercy till they reach the field,
> And deal brave blows beside him. All in vain:
> It is too late. Alas, they come too late!

The poem here consists mainly of descriptions of single combats, characterized by ferocity on one side and prowess on the other. We pass on to the death of Oliver.

> When Roland sees the cursèd heathen folk,
> As black as ink — all black except their teeth —
> He says: "Our death is certain. Frenchmen, strike!
> Woe to the laggards!" and his men all rush
> Into the conflict. . . .

Oliver, overpowered and mortally wounded, kills his adversary, the Caliph, and then calls Roland to the rescue, who, when he sees his friend dying, mourns over him, and faints away on his horse.

> Behold now Roland fainting on his horse;
> And Oliver, whose life is ebbing fast.
> His eyes are dim, he does not know his friend,

And rides to his encounter, dealing him,
Full on his gilded helm, a dreadful blow.
It cleaves the helmet, and lays bare his brow.
The shock restores his consciousness. He says,
Full gently : " Comrade, did you mean to strike ?
'Tis Roland, Roland, whom you hold so dear.
You had not challenged me to fight with you."
"I hear you, Roland," answered Oliver,
"I cannot see you, but I pray to God
To have you in His sight. For that rude blow
I pray you pardon me." But Roland said :
"You did not wound me. Here and before God
I do forgive you." Then they bowed them low,
Each to the other. In this way they part,
Courteous and loving.

  Oliver, feeling that his death is near,
Dismounts, and lying low upon the ground,
Confesses all his sins, and lifts joined hands,
Imploring God to grant him paradise,
To bless sweet France, and Charles the Emperor,
And Roland above all men. Then he dies.
 . . . . .
The noble Roland, when he sees his friend
Lying face downward, prone along the ground,
Cannot forbear from sighing and from tears.
Full low he speaks, and thus bewails himself :
" Companion, to thy cost thou wert so bold.
We have been comrades many years and days.
Thou never didst me harm, nor harmed I thee.
Since thou art dead, I sorrow that I live."
And saying this, the Marquis faints away
Upon his horse, well known as Veillantif.
His golden spurs are fastened to his heels
He cannot fall.

  A whirlwind sweeps over the land of France,
Terrific tempests and great thunder-gusts,
And hail and rain in torrents. It is said,
And said with truth, there was an earthquake felt

> From Mount St. Michael to the holy shrine
> In far Cologne. As well from Besançon
> To western port of Wishant. Not a house
> But shook to its foundations, and at noon
> Darkness profound. Save where the lightning came,
> Cleaving the sky, there was no light at all.
> All who beheld these portents quaked with fear,
> And many said, " It is the Judgment-day ;
> It is the end of the world." They little knew
> 'Twas the great mourning for the death of Roland.

When Roland comes to himself, he sees the extent of the disaster. Only two of his knights are left, Gautier of Hum, and the Archbishop, both mortally wounded, the Archbishop in four places. Roland has dragged him out of the conflict, and has driven off the Saracens for the time. He lays the prelate gently upon the grass, binds up his wounds, and begs of him one last service — to bless the dead as he had blessed the living.

> Roland departs. He searches all the field
> He searches lofty crags and valleys deep;
> He finds Ivon and Ivory, Gérin,
> Gérier, his friend the Gascon Engelers;
> He finds Gérart, the old of Roussillon,
> Bérenger, Othon, Samson, and Anselm.
> He brings them one by one, and lays them down,
> At Turpin's feet he lays them in a row.
> The good Archbishop cannot choose but weep.
> He lifts his hand, and blesses them from God.
> " Fair sirs," said he, " you came in evil hour.
> May God, all-glorious, rest your souls in peace
> In holy flowers in heaven ! Alas for me !
> The pains of death encompass me about
> I never more shall see the Emperor."

Roland looks for Oliver's body, and brings it, held close to his heart, to receive also the Archbishop's benediction; and after bewailing his loss and reciting his friend's virtues, he faints away again. The Archbishop tries to restore him, but dies in the attempt. At last Roland comes to himself alone.

> When Roland sees the Archbishop is dead,
> He crosses on his breast his fair white hands,
> And then aloud, the fashion of his land,
> He makes his orison : "Ah, gentlemen,
> Most noble knight, I leave you to the care
> Of the All-glorious One who dwells above.
> You served your master gladly. Never man
> Since the apostles was a greater prophet
> To keep the faith and draw men after him.
> God grant your soul, set free,
> Through open doors may pass to paradise!"
>
> Then Roland feels that his own death is near.
> His brains ooze through his ears. He says his prayers,
> First for his friends to God, to Gabriel,
> Commends his soul, then takes the olifant
> In one hand, in the other Durandal.
> Thus all equipped, he goes a bow-shot's length,
> Far as an arbalète can send a stone,
> On Spanish soil. He climbs a little hill
> In a wide field. There, under two fine trees,
> Lie four great blocks of marble. Roland falls
> Back on the greensward, and then faints away.
> Death is at hand. Aoi!

A Saracen is lying on the ground not far off, who has covered his face with blood, feigning death. He leaps to his feet, and cries exultingly: "He is conquered, Charlemagne's great nephew! I shall take his sword back with me to Arabia." He seizes Durandal, and pulls Roland's beard. At this indignity the hero comes to himself, and dashes the Saracen's brains out with his olifant. He then tries to break Durandal to pieces against the stones, but in vain. Thus he mourns over his sword:

>"O my good Durandal! how fair and bright
>Thou flamest in the sunshine! Charlemagne
>In the Savoyard valleys heard from heaven
>(An angel told him) that it was a gift
>For a great captain. Then the noble King
>Girded it at my side. . . .
>Have I not conquered towns and lands enough
>That own the sway of Charles with the white beard?
>And now my grief is great for this good sword.
>I cannot leave it for these pagan folk.
>Lord God our Father, bring not France to shame!"
>Now Roland feels the death-chill at his heart.
>He runs and throws himself beneath a pine,
>Face downward on the greensward. Under him
>He puts his good sword and his olifant,
>And turns his face toward the heathen host.
>Why does he thus? That Charles and all the French
>May see he died a conqueror. Aoi!
>
>He lies upon the hill o'erlooking Spain,
>And beats his breast with one hand, and he cries:
>"Lord, I have greatly sinned in Thy pure sight.
>Mercy for all the great and little sins,
>All I have done since I was born till now!"
>Holds out the glove of his right hand to God.
>Angels from heaven descend and hover near.

The French arrive, and find the ground strewed with the bodies of their friends and foes.

>The Emperor, in searching far and wide,
>At last espied a meadow where the grass
>And flowers were blood-stained. As he rode,
>For pity the great King shed bitter tears.
>And when he reached the height beneath the trees,
>And knew the strokes of Roland on the stones,
>And saw his nephew lying on the grass,

It is no marvel that his grief was great.
He left his horse, and ran to where he lay,
Lifted him up, and then, in dire distress,
Fainted away.

The Emperor recovers from his swoon;
Four of his barons hold him by the hand.
But he looks down and sees where Roland lies,
His eyes upturned and full of darkness, pale,
So ghastly pale, but still a gallant man.
And thus he mourns him in great faith and love:
" Friend Roland, may God rest thy soul in flowers
Among the blessèd saints in paradise!
Ill did betide thee when thou cam'st to Spain.
Each day I live shall be new grief for me;
My power, my joy, my pride, all gone with thee!
Who will sustain me in my kingdom? None.
Where are my friends? The only one is dead.
My kin? There is not one of them like him."
Great handfuls of his hair the King tears out.
A hundred thousand Frenchmen stand around,
And every one lets fall some scalding tears.

"Friend Roland, I shall hie me back to France,
And when I come to my good town of Laon,
Strangers shall journey there from many realms
And ask me of my famous captain. Then
I shall make answer: 'He has died in Spain.'
In sorrow I shall reign, and every day
Shall groan and weep for thee, Roland, my friend.

"Friend Roland, valiant man and beauteous youth,
When I betake me to Aix-la-Chapelle,
And men shall come to ask for news of thee,
All I can say is cruel. He is dead,
My nephew whom I loved, my conqueror!
And now the Saxons will rebel again,
And many other peoples, Africans,
Sicilians, those of Hungary, La Pouille,
And far Bulgaria. Where is the Count?
Who now can lead my armies? He is dead
Who led to victory. Each day I live

I suffer more. O my sweet land of France,
Behold you orphaned! Bitter is my grief.
I do not care to live." Then with both hands
He tears his beard and hair. The Frenchmen fall,
A hundred thousand fainting to the ground.

Charlemagne chases the Saracens across the Ebro, defeats them with great slaughter, and takes Saragossa, where a hundred thousand heathen prefer Christian baptism to a violent death. Marsile dies of wounds received in battle, his son is killed, and his wife Braminonde is taken prisoner. Roland thus avenged, the Emperor returns to Aix la-Chapelle, where he is met in the hall of his palace by the beautiful Alda, or Aude, Oliver's sister, and the betrothed of Roland.

Charles, the great King, has just arrived from Spain;
Journeys to Aix, that famous town of France;
Goes to his palace; in the entrance-hall
Is met by Alda, and the ladye fair
Asks: "Where is Roland, the great captain? where
Is he who swore to take me for his wife?"
The Emperor, bowed down with heavy grief,
Bursts into tears, and tears his snowy beard.
"Sister, dear friend, you ask for a dead man.
All I can do is this: In Roland's place
Take Louis for your husband, Louis my son,
Who keeps the Marches. More I cannot do."
"These are strange words, my liege," Alda replies.
"May God and all His saints and angels grant
That, Roland dead, I may no longer live!"
Deadly her pallor, at the Emperor's feet
Lifeless she falls. Alda the fair is dead.
May God in heaven have mercy on her soul!
For pity the French barons wondering weep.

The lovely Alda to her rest has gone,
But Charles believes that she has only swooned.
He weeps for pity as he looks at her,

THE SONG OF ROLAND 59

> Then lifts her up and takes her by the hand.
> The fair head droops, and now the Emperor
> Knows that she is dead. Four noble ladies come
> (So the King orders), and they bear her forth
> Hard by unto a convent. There they watch
> Beside the maiden till the morning breaks.
> Then she is buried in great pomp and state
> Close to the altar: such the King's command.

Excepting Braminonde, wife of Marsile, Alda is the only woman mentioned in the "Song of Roland," and the little glimpse of her is a touching one. The position of both is noticeable. The word used for wife by Alda, when she says, "Roland, who swore to take me for his wife," is *per*, translated *femme* in the modern French versions, not unlike our word *peer*. Braminonde is quite the type of a Southern heroine, ardent and active, devoted to her own people. She helps bribe Ganelon with magnificent bracelets of her own, which the traitor hides in his boot or hose. She urges the Saracens to fight instead of fleeing before the vengeful Charlemagne, and seems to mourn her husband's defeat even more than his death. In the end she becomes a Christian of her own free-will while a prisoner in France.

The trial of Ganelon at Aix is a very interesting piece of legal procedure according to the Teutonic forms of the time. First, arrest and corporeal punishment before the "placitum palatii," the trial proper, presided over by the King, who, however, has no voice in the assembly. The process ends with an appeal to the judgment of God in the ordeal by battle, or deadly combat. Ganelon's champion falls, and he himself is therefore condemned to die the death of a traitor, torn asunder by four wild horses. His thirty sureties are all hung at the same time. This traitor baron is no villain of the ordinary stamp, but a bold, brave man meant for better things, who falls a prey at last to his fierce envy and vindictive, jealous hatred of Roland, his son-in-law.

The Emperor is weary and worn with grief, though Ganelon's sentence and Braminonde's conversion have comforted him a little. Finally he has a vision, commanding him to go to the help of distressed Christians in a place that bears the mysterious name of "Imphes." The Crusades are impending.

Thus ends the "Song of Roland," honest in its reverence, pure though rough in its expression (there is not a single coarse word in it from beginning to end); a Christian poem, the story of a signal defeat that becomes an inspiration for a great triumph. It is eminently serious in its tone, the only comic part being that where Ganelon is chained up like a tame bear, and given over to the King's scullions to be beaten with rods. This gayety has been truly said to savor more of camps than courts. There is a supernatural flavor throughout: Charlemagne is warned in dreams; he bids the sun stand still like Joshua, and is obeyed: angels stoop over the dying Roland and help the Emperor to avenge his loss.

Roland dies as a hero and a martyr; but greater than his affection for the Church is his love of France. Dreading lest Durandal should fall into pagan hands after his death, he prays, "O Lord God our Father, let not France be brought to shame." We can but wonder with a recent French writer that his countrymen for full three hundred years allowed such a poem as this to be ignored and forgotten, — one that embodies the national life of the time, preserving, moreover, types that no one can fail to recognize to-day. For is not the undisciplined, rash, haughty courage of Roland still dear to the heart of the French nation? Does not his passion for "France, sweet France, France the free," yet find an echo there?

As Heine's grenadier grieves over the "forsaken emperor" more than for wife and child, so it is Oliver and not Roland who speaks of Alda in the conflict. The hero's last prayer is for France, and not for his ladye.

Many people, says Ludlow (we quote the substance of his remarks) who admire French prose, but condemn French literature as unpoetical, do not know that in the tenth and eleventh centuries, far behind Froissart, there lies in the French language a group of poems unsurpassed as a whole in European literature. Of these the oldest, the most complete, and the most beautiful is the "Song of Roland."

It is founded on historic fact, overlaid with fiction, and illuminated with legend. There were really two or three disasters at Roncesvaux; the first in the days of Dagobert, and another, related by Eginhard in the ninth chapter of his *Life of Charlemagne*. In a recently discovered MS. of the National Library in Paris we read as follows:

"On the 15th of August, 778, Charlemagne, retiring from Spain, where his campaign had been only partially successful, gave the command of his rear-guard to Roland, his nephew, to protect his march through the Pyrenean passes. Close to the place where the chapel of Ibagneta now stands, in the pass of Roncesvaux, the rear-guard was attacked and cut to pieces by the Gascon mountaineers, Roland himself being killed."

Michel, in his edition of the "Song of Roland," gives this "Song of Alta-biçar" as a commemoration of the event in popular Basque poetry. Whether authentic or not, it is remarkable for its rude vigor.

"A cry has arisen from the midst of the mountains of the Escualdanac, and the master of the house, standing before his door, has opened his ears, and said, 'Who goes there? What will they with me?' And the dog that slept at his master's feet has roused itself, and has filled the neighborhood of Alta-biçar with its barkings.

"In the pass of Ibagneta a noise resounds; it nears, touching the rocks to right, to left; it is the dull murmur of a coming army. Our men have replied to it from the mountain-tops; they have blown in their ox-horns, and the master of the house sharpens his arrows.

"They come! they come! What a hedge of spears! How the rainbow-hued banners float in the midst! What lightning flashes from their weapons! How many are there? Child, reckon them well. 'One, two, three, four, five, six, seven, eight, nine, ten, eleven, twelve, thirteen, fourteen, fifteen, sixteen, seventeen, eighteen, nineteen, twenty.'

"Twenty, and thousands more besides! One should lose time in reckoning them. Let us unite our sinewy arms; let us uproot these rocks; let us fling them from the mountain-tops upon their very heads! Crush them! kill them!

"And what had they to do in our mountains, these men of the North? Why are they come to disturb our peace? When God makes mountains, it is that men may not cross them. But the rocks fall rolling, they overwhelm the troops; blood streams, flesh quivers. Oh, how many crushed bones! What a sea of blood!

"Flee, flee, all to whom strength remains and a horse. Flee, King Karloman, with thy black plumes and thy red mantle. Thy nephew, thy bravest, thy darling Roland, is stretched dead yonder. His courage was of no avail. And now, Escualdanac, let us leave the rocks there, let us quickly descend, flinging our arrows at the fugitives.

"They flee, they flee. Where now is the hedge of spears?—where the rainbow-hued banners floating in their midst? Lightnings flash no more from their blood-soiled weapons. How many are there? Child, reckon them well. Twenty, nineteen, eighteen, seventeen, sixteen, fifteen, fourteen, thirteen, twelve, eleven, ten, nine, eight, seven, six, five, four, three, two, one?

"One! There is not even one. It is done. Master of the house, you may go in with your dogs, kiss wife and children, clean your arrows, put them away with your ox-horn, then lie down over them to sleep. By night the eagles shall come and eat the crushed flesh, and the bones shall whiten in eternity."

The popularity of the legend would seem to show that the defeat was a more important one than the brief historical mention would indicate. The "Song of Roland" itself is founded on these words of Eginhard: "In this disaster perished Hruolandus, prefect of the marches of Brittany."

This poem is written in lines of ten syllables, the heroic pentameter, with the break after the fourth syllable. It is divided into "laisses," or stanzas of twelve or fifteen lines in almost every instance, all the lines of each stanza ending with the same vowel sound. And this assocance, as it is called, is not meant for the eye, but for the ear. It should be borne in mind that the poem was meant to be sung or recited.

Almost all the stanzas end with a mysterious, untranslatable word — *aoi*. At one time it was thought to be a war-cry, and this accorded with the Taillefer story; but then it was said to be an old musical notation; and there was another theory that it is a sort of wailing refrain, like the *ahe*, or *ay*, at the end of many old lyrics in all the Romance languages.

The mourning for Roland has been thought to remind one of the passage in the Georgics describing the omens of Cæsar's death. The enumeration of the French and Saracen nobles, and of the different peoples that composed the heathen host, is Homeric, as well as the constantly recurring epithets, and the vast amount of single combats that make up the battles; but our trouvère, probably a Norman of the eleventh century, most likely knew nothing of Homer or Virgil.

Roland is a cosmopolite. A valuable MS. copy of the poem is extant in Venice, and our hero has stood in stone with his friend and companion in arms, Oliver, at the doorway of the cathedral in Verona for seven hundred years.

Pulci, Aretino, and Ariosto have all sung of his renown. Our Shakespeare knew the two friends, and has handed down to us "a Roland for an Oliver." There is an English version of the poem, dating from the thirteenth century. Germany has her "Ruolandusliet" and the Icelandic peasant of Reikiavik can recount the deeds of Roland. In Denmark and the Netherlands the story is popular, and the Spanish version most in vogue relates that the nephew of the great Emperor was defeated by Bernardo del Carpio. According to Gautier, while all nations of Europe have been delighted to copy or translate this Iliad, literary France in the sixteenth century became so absorbed in Æneas that she forgot Roland, and this ingratitude has lasted three hundred years. In 1836, however, M. Francisque Michel installed himself in the Bodleian Library and brought out the first French edition from that famous Oxford MS. Since then there has been a revival of interest in old French, and our poem bids fair to be again popular in the land of its birth. We cannot feel as we lay it down that the "great century" of Louis the Fourteenth, or the Second Empire either, is all there is of French literature.

BEAUMARCHAIS

At a brilliant *fête* given by the city of Paris to the first Napoleon, the emperor suddenly paused, in his progress through the gay crowd, in front of a pretty woman with an animated, eager face, and asked her name. Her answer was simply this: " I am the daughter of Beaumarchais." Have we any idea of the just pride with which those words were uttered, or can we feel how much they meant to him who heard them? It may answer for the world at large to remember only that Beaumarchais was the author of the " Barber of Seville," and the witty defendant in some famous lawsuits; but students of our early history are aware of his claims to the grateful remembrance of American citizens, ignored and controverted though those claims have been.

The only boy in a family of six children, Pierre Augustin Caron, better known as Beaumarchais, was born in Paris in 1732, the year of Washington's birth. Undreamed of then, it is rarely recalled now, that the one was to supplement the other; that the opportune, sorely needed succor sent by Beaumarchais from France for our brave men at Valley Forge cheered the sinking heart of the great general in that darkest hour before dawn. Beaumarchais died convinced that we were utterly ungrateful. Is it true, and if true can we afford to remain so?

That was a humble home in the Rue St. Denis, where the watchmaker, his father, dwelt; but hardly in our own favored land could one be found more affectionate, more cultivated, or more refined in its atmosphere. There were five sisters to pet and admire the only brother among them, and at fifteen Pierre would seem to have been a lively, spoiled child, devoted to music, in which he excelled, and fond of playing pranks and writing verses instead of working steadily at his father's trade, to which he was apprenticed. Music, indeed, must have been a family gift. All the children played on one or more instruments, and composed accompaniments to the little songs which they wrote on various festive occasions; for there was evidently a great deal of fun and fondness, as well as accomplishment and cultivation, in this watchmaker's home. One sister, Julia, understood Italian and Spanish well, and enjoyed the writings of Young and Richardson. Her letters are very graceful and lively, and she became in later life an author. Like her brother, however, her character is more remarkable than her writings.

The father was of good Huguenot stock, but had signed his public recantation before Pierre was born. It must be remembered that he could not otherwise have established himself in business in Paris, such was the prevalent intolerance even in those days of indifference and scepticism. When his son was hardly eighteen, his father turned him out of doors for idleness and dissipation; keeping an eye upon him all the time, however, and conspiring with some friends who went to the rescue of the boy. The following letter, in which the father consents to the return of the contrite prodigal, throws some light on the relation between parents and children in those days: —

"Your great misfortune consists in my having lost all confidence in you. Nevertheless, the esteem and friendship which I feel for the excellent people who have befriended you, and the gratitude I owe them for their kindness, induce me to consent to your return, persuaded though I am that there is hardly any chance that you will keep your word. These are my conditions: (1) That you shall make, sell, or cause to be made or sold, absolutely nothing, except for me alone. You shall not sell even an old watch-key without rendering an account of it to me. (2) You must get up in summer at six, and in winter at seven. You must work cheerfully till supper-time at anything I give you to do. I mean that you shall employ the ability God has given you to become famous in your profession. Remember that it is shameful and disgraceful not to excel, and that if you do not become eminent you forfeit my respect; for the love of such a noble art should penetrate your heart, and fill your mind to the exclusion of all other interests. (3) You must not go out any more to supper, or stay away from home of an evening; but you may dine with your friends on Sundays and holidays, on condition, however, that I know where you go, and that you always come back before nine o'clock. (4) You must give up entirely your *miserable music*, and, above all, the society of other young men. Both these things have brought you to ruin. Nevertheless, through regard to your weakness, I allow you to play on the flute and violin; but only on the express condition that it shall be in the evening on week-days, and at such times and places, moreover, as shall not interfere with our neighbors' rest, or my own either."

The boy promised to obey, and faithfully kept his word. From this time he never seems to have forfeited his father's esteem or affection; on the contrary, he became the pride and joy of his life. Two years after, he invented a tiny escapement for watches, but was robbed of all honor and profit for the time being by the dishonesty of a well-known watchmaker of the city, in whom he had with pride confided, and who appropriated the invention. The lad prosecuted him, however, and finally triumphed. The suit had attracted attention, and soon after he was appointed watchmaker to the king. Then he made a watch with the new escapement as a present for Madame Pompadour, who wore it in a ring on her finger. Such watches became the fashion, and orders flowed in from all the courtiers and those who mimicked their ways. Among these customers came a lady whose husband, considerably older than herself, held a place in the king's household. Enchanted with the young man's appearance and manner, she cultivated his acquaintance, put him in the way of buying her husband's place at court, when he gave it up soon afterwards, and, on the old man's death, married the handsome young watchmaker. From a small estate in her possession he now assumed the name of Beaumarchais, which he shared at once with his favorite sister, Julia. He became also, about this time, secretary to his majesty, — rather a sinecure, one would think, in this part of the reign of Louis XV., — and soon made himself indispensable to the princesses, those four royal ladies whose pious, retired life in the centre of the gay, licentious court of their father, presented such a striking contrast to their surroundings. Beaumarchais taught them to play on everything, from a trombone to a jew's-harp; procured them all the instruments they wanted; organized and presided at the weekly entertainments they gave their father — concerts attended by the queen, the dauphin, and all the best part of the court. The thoughtlessness of the princesses in money matters, or their inability to pay for the instruments he bought for their use, was an endless source of embarrassment to their *protégé*, whose means were far from unlimited. However, he was making his way. The dauphin liked the young man, and said once, "Beaumarchais is the only person who speaks the truth to me." After his untimely death, no doubt, this partiality was an additional passport to his sisters' favor.

The story of the watch has been often told, but may bear repetition. One day a young noble stopped Beaumarchais, as, all arrayed in his court suit, he was passing through the palace corridor, on his way to give a lesson to his royal pupils, and asked him, with mock gravity, to examine his watch, and see what was the matter with it. A group of youthful aristocrats at once drew near to enjoy the sport. "I should not advise you to trust it in my hands," said the young aspirant. "I have grown very awkward." His tormentor insisting, with profuse compliments, much to the amusement of his friends, Beaumarchais lifted the watch up to the light, as if to look closely at it, and then dropped it deliberately on the ground, so that it was crushed by the fall. Turning on his heel, saying, "I told you I had grown very awkward," he left the disconcerted courtier to pick up the pieces himself. Then he fought a duel, and killed another young nobleman who had insulted him, but was too generous to reveal the name of his adversary before he died of his wounds.

He now persuaded his father, perhaps on account of all this trouble, to close his shop, and take up his abode with him. The old man did so reluctantly, but never seems to have repented of his acquiescence.

Through his influence with the king's daughters, he ingratiated himself with an old speculator and financier, Paris Duverny, who had helped Voltaire to make his fortune, and was ready to do the same for young Beaumarchais. They entered into partnership, made extensive business arrangements, and set on foot many projects, almost always with a view to public benefit as well as private profit.

Meantime, two of Beaumarchais' sisters had gone to Madrid, where one married an architect, and the younger became affianced to a literary man in favor at the Spanish court. Twice, when the wedding-day had been fixed and all preparations completed, the bridegroom had not been forthcoming, and the second time he failed to appear the young girl was made alarmingly ill by distress and mortification. Learning this, her brother first assured himself that she was in no wise to blame, and then departed post haste for Madrid, sought an interview with the faithless lover, and, on his refusing satisfaction, left no stone unturned till he had procured his public disgrace and summary dismissal. Goethe has made this story the subject of a play entitled "Clavigo," in which he introduces Beaumarchais as "the avenger." Our hero remained a year in Madrid, where he made many friends, came into high favor at court, and contracted an intimacy with Lord Rochford, the English ambassador. Here again his "miserable music" made the bond of sympathy and contributed to his advancement.

He proposed at this time to colonize the Sierra Morena, to take the place of commissary-general of the king's army, and also, I regret to say, obtained a monopoly for supplying the Spanish West India Islands with negroes direct from Africa. This project, however, seems ultimately to have been abandoned. His next step was to purchase a new place at court, that of *lieutenant général des chasses*, or superintendent of the king's hunting grounds. This office involved the exercise of judicial functions, and now we find him invested with robes of state, holding court every week at the Palais de Justice.

He had lost his wife about a year after their marriage,

and on his return from Spain there had been a projected union with a certain fair West Indian ward, in whom he was greatly interested, and who had become an inmate of his family. But this affair never culminated, and Beaumarchais soon married another widow, beautiful, brilliant, and very rich. She died in three years, and their little son did not long survive her.

At this time he first appeared in the character of a dramatic author. His two plays, "Eugène" and "Les Deux Amis," met with no great success, and added nothing to his reputation; they were of the sentimental, serious character then in vogue, and are now forgotten. The most conspicuous part he then played was that of a wood merchant. In partnership with M. Paris-Duverny he had bought the great forest of Chinon, and they were engaged in this business on a large scale, when M. Duverny died, and their accounts remained unsettled. Unfortunately, a nephew of the old financier, the Comte de la Blache, an avowed enemy of Beaumarchais, was appointed executor and residuary legatee. All Beaumarchais' claims against the estate were contested, litigation ensued, and when the first decision was rendered against him, the count appealed to a higher court, in which a commoner would necessarily contend at great disadvantage with a member of the aristocracy. The refusal to accept Beaumarchais' statements involved an accusation of forgery, and while this important suit remained undecided a great scandal occurred. A brutal, stalwart nobleman, the Duc de Chaulnes, had become jealous of the favor shown Beaumarchais by a young actress whom the duke had taken under his protection. She appears to have been frightened by the nobleman's violence, and he attributed her changed manner to the successful rivalship of our hero, challenged him to fight a duel, and, while they were waiting for their seconds, made an assault upon him in his own house, literally with tooth and nail. The police was obliged to interfere, and both parties were arrested. The duke was sent to Vincennes, and Beaumarchais to a less distinguished place of confinement, where he remained a long time, to the great detriment of his lawsuit.

The stanch old Parliament of Paris had been exiled, and was now replaced by the servile assembly called, from its creator, the Maupeou Parliament. It shows the frivolous mood of those days, that when one of the members of this assembly complained to Maurepas that they could not show themselves in the streets without being insulted by the populace, the minister replied, "Wear dominos, then, and they will not know you." To a member of this discredited and most discreditable body was referred the suit brought by the Comte de la Blache against Beaumarchais. It was a serious matter, affecting his character no less than his property. Beaumarchais received permission to leave his place of confinement, attended by a jailer, in order to solicit his judges, as was customary. But he failed in his repeated attempts to see the counsellor Goëzman, whom he had reason to believe prejudiced against him by persistent endeavors, made by friends of La Blache and the Duke de Chaulnes, to blacken his character. They had published and widely disseminated most atrocious libels and unfounded accusations against him; among others, that of poisoning his two wives. In this dilemma, unable to obtain an audience, it was suggested that a handsome present made to Madame Goëzman, wife of the counsellor, might gain him admission to the husband's presence.

The experiment was tried, and it succeeded, though the interview was unsatisfactory, and the decision, when rendered, proved to be adverse. It had been agreed that if the suit were decided against him the lady should return the money given her; and she did so, all but a small sum, fifteen louis, said to be retained as a compensation to the great man's secretary. Beaumarchais discovered that this individual had never received the money, and he immediately wrote to Madame Goëzman, indignantly demanding restitution. Probably having spent the money, she complained to her husband; and he, possibly misinformed in regard to the details of the affair, prosecuted Beaumarchais at once for false accusation and endeavor to corrupt a magistrate in the exercise of his judicial functions. Publicity in legal affairs was then unknown in France, such cases always being tried with closed doors, and Beaumarchais knew that Goëzman could thus bid him defiance with perfect impunity in the Maupeou Parliament. In this extremity, on the brink of financial ruin, his property attached for the debt to the Duverny estate, his hands tied, and his character defamed by libels industriously circulated, he had the genius to perceive that his only salvation lay in dealing a deadly blow at the infamous power, the assembly, which had pronounced one verdict against him, and most likely would hasten to confirm it by another. There was a great risk to be run; for the king himself would be indirectly assaulted in the persons of these members, his subservient tools; but what else could be done? No one could be found to undertake his case, so he became his own advocate, and proved a most able one. In polite European society, for the next seven months, his brilliant defence of himself and his scathing assaults of his enemies were the staple topics of conversation and an unfailing source of amusement.

Voltaire, Horace Walpole, and Goethe have all recorded their delight in these Memorials. The gay young dauphiness, Marie Antoinette, enjoyed them extremely, and named the bunch of plumes that crowned her head-dress from a jest in one of his dramatic reports of the proceedings. These witty appeals to public opinion, in which he knew "how to merge his private grievances in the public wrongs," and to hold up for merciless ridicule a deservedly despised tribunal, introduced publicity in legal affairs, and made certain the downfall of the hated Parliament. It was not, however, legally abolished till 1774. A wit of the day said, "It took Louis Quinze to establish, and *quinze louis* to overthrow, the Maupeou Parliament." At the end of a seven-months' contest with a private individual, this notorious body signed its own death-warrant by condemning both Beaumarchais and the counsellor Goëzman to "public censure." They were declared to have forfeited their civil rights, and the famous Memorials were ordered to be burned by the public executioner. When the verdict was made known it became the signal for a perfect ovation. All people of distinction in Paris flocked to the house of Beaumarchais, and vied in doing him honor. Led by the Prince de Conti, the world of fashion waited on the condemned criminal, and he was entitled "the first citizen of France," from a well-known passage in his Memorials, in which he says, "I am a citizen, and I mean by that neither a courtier, an abbé, a man of rank, a financier, or a favorite. I am a citizen; that is to say, what you should have been for the last two hundred years,—what you may be, perhaps, in twenty years to come."

One statesman at this time laughingly warned him that it was not enough to have been sentenced by the Maupeou Parliament; he must try and bear his honors meekly.

The keen satire, fun, and graphic descriptions of these Memorials have secured for them a permanent place in French literature. All the scenes in which he introduces Madame Goëzman are particularly comic. She was a frivolous, pretty woman, whose head was turned by a compliment, and who became hopelessly bewildered in her statements. She shows in her conduct a remarkable mixture of craft, innocence, and impudence. "The poor woman," confronted with Beaumarchais, is made to say black is white; he alternately soothes and enrages her. When he drives her distracted, she threatens to box his ears; when he pays her a compliment, and says that he should take her to be eighteen instead of thirty, she smiles in spite of herself, does not think him quite so impertinent, and even asks him to escort her to her carriage. It is the gayest, most delicious irony. As he says to himself, "Cry as much as you may, you cannot help laughing. Je suis un peu comme la cousine d'Héloïse, j'ai beau pleurer, il faut toujours que le rire s'échappe par quelque coin." Some passages of a different sort have become classic; for instance, the one ending with this prayer: "Being of Beings, I owe thee all: the joy of living, of thinking and feeling. I believe that thou hast ordered good and evil for us in equal measure. I believe that thy justice wisely compensates us for all, and that the succession of pain and pleasure, of fear and hope, is the fresh wind which fills the vessel's sails, and sends her gayly on her way."

Though a popular idol, he was yet legally disfranchised, and Beaumarchais was not a man to resign himself to his fate except for the time being, — "*provisoirement,*" as he says. He had just married, too, for the third time. His wife was a most estimable and attractive woman, who was full of enthusiasm for the hero of the Goëzman suit, and he was unwearied in his endeavors to procure his restoration to civil rights by ingratiating himself with Louis XV. He undertook, among other things, a delicate diplomatic mission, and induced an unscrupulous scoundrel, who had taken refuge in England, to forego the publication of some scandalous memoirs of Madame Du Barry. This was accomplished "for a consideration;" but when Beaumarchais returned to claim his reward, Louis XV. was on his death-bed, and his labor had been all in vain. Nothing daunted, however, he undertook to manage the mysterious Chevalier d'Eon for the new king, gained his point, and then offered to obtain the suppression of a pamphlet, offensive to Marie Antoinette, which was in the possession of a certain Jew named Angelucci. His remarkable adventures with Jews and bandits, his kind reception by Maria Theresa, and his subsequent incarceration in Austria are amusingly related by Loménie. While in England, employed in these delicate diplomatic missions, he had renewed his intimacy with his Madrid friend, Lord Rochford, now a cabinet minister, and he had become also a frequent visitor at the house of John Wilkes. There he met many of the friends of America, and subsequently made the acquaintance of the man who was destined to do him so much harm, Arthur Lee. France was at this time in a state of great exasperation against England, and Beaumarchais tried with all his might for two years to convince Louis XVI. of what he fully believed himself, — that civil war was imminent across the Channel, that the attempt to coerce America was extremely unpopular, and that aiding the insurgents would insure the final destruction of the dreaded hereditary enemy of France. To injure England, and thus aggrandize his own country, was apparently his object at first ; but as he learned more of our struggle for liberty, he evidently became deeply interested in the issue.

In 1776, Congress sent Silas Deane to Paris to solicit aid for our dauntless army. Before any answer could arrive from him, the secret committee of Congress received a communication from Arthur Lee, in London, stating that the French ambassador at the court of St. James had been won over to the American cause by his strenuous efforts and powerful persuasion, and, at his solicitation, had induced his government to send a secret agent to him, Arthur Lee, offering as a gratuity a million livres. This present, however, he added, was to be made under cover of a commercial transaction of some kind, for fear of alarming England, with whom France was then at peace.

The truth was that the French ambassador in London knew nothing at all of the matter, and that Beaumarchais, striving to interest Louis XVI. and his ministers in what he had learned to regard as a great and glorious cause, had merely called on Arthur Lee, and imparted to him his own scheme for conveying assistance to the colonies. Indeed, in urgent letters to M. Vergennes on this subject, of a subsequent date, he alludes to Mr. Lee as an American who will go to Paris, and confer with the ministers, if they eventually consent to help America.

The enthusiastic advocacy and persistent energy of Beaumarchais at last produced an effect. The king agreed to aid the "insurgents," but on the express condition that the commercial transaction should be *bona fide*. Beaumarchais on his part agreed to establish in Paris a mercantile house, under the assumed name of Rodrigue Hortalez & Co., for the purpose of procuring and sending to America all sorts of military supplies, to be paid for, on long credit, by returns of American products. This plan entirely superseded the first idea of gratuitous help, and met with especial favor, as it seemed to obviate the danger of war with England.

When, therefore, Silas Deane made his application for aid, it was refused; but at the same time he was given to understand that he could doubtless make advantageous arrangements with the house of Hortalez & Co. It had been settled that arms, ammunition, and all sorts of military stores could be taken from the royal arsenals, — to be returned, however; and also that his majesty should stand between the colonists and their creditor, to see that they were not pressed for speedy payment.

How the house of Rodrigue Hortalez & Co. should be subsidized, if at all, by the French government, would seem clearly to have been a matter between Beaumarchais and the ministers. But, strangely enough, in after years, this idea appears never to have occurred to congressional committees, who persistently refused to pay Beaumarchais till they had found out all about his transactions with his own government.

Beaumarchais, finding Silas Deane the accredited American agent in Paris, now made all his arrangements with him on the new basis, perfectly unaware of the unfounded expectations which had been excited by Lee, whose premature statement to Congress was refuted by the actual condition of things, and who found himself, moreover, quite overshadowed by Deane. Lee now tried to maintain his ground and revenge himself by representing, in his correspondence with his influential relatives at home, that Beaumarchais was an unscrupulous, intriguing adventurer, who was trying to enrich himself out of the king's free gift ; and that Silas Deane had been entrapped by him, and induced to join in the plot. Distance and the medium of an imperfectly understood foreign language made this tangled web very hard to unravel.

Dr. Franklin, too, who had just arrived as joint commissioner with Silas Deane and Arthur Lee, was prejudiced against Beaumarchais, and a strange oversight of his own contributed not a little to keep up the mystification for many years to come. Dr. Dubourg, an old gentleman, who was a warm friend of America, and who had translated the Declaration of Independence into French, to Dr. Franklin's great delight, dissatisfied to see himself thus overshadowed and supplanted by Beaumarchais, wrote to M. de Vergennes : " I have seen M. Beaumarchais this morning, and have conferred with him. No one does more justice than myself to his honesty, discretion, and zeal for all that is great and good. I believe him to be the best man in the world for political negotiations, but perhaps at the same time the most unfitted for commercial transactions. He likes show, and I am assured that he supports several young women. . . . There is not in all France a merchant or a manufacturer who would not hesitate to have business dealings with him."

The minister, infinitely amused, sent the letter at

once to Beaumarchais himself, who thus answers the doctor : —

> MY DEAR SIR, — Grant that I am wasteful and extravagant, and support young women : how does that affect the matter in hand ? The young women whom I have supported for the last twenty years are your very humble servants. They were five in number, four sisters and one niece. Three years ago two of these young women died, to my great regret, and now I support only three, two sisters and one niece. No doubt this is extravagant for a private person like me. But what would you have thought, if, knowing me better, you had become aware of the outrageous fact that I have supported men also, two young nephews, — pretty fellows, — and even the unfortunate father who brought into the world such a scandalous supporter?

This Dubourg episode shows conclusively that the commercial character of the transaction was fully recognized and acknowledged, in France at least.

Beaumarchais now went to work at his chosen task with such hearty good-will and abounding energy that before one year had elapsed he had transmitted supplies to the amount of a million livres. Acting under the misconception, however, of supposing it all a free gift from the King of France, Congress sent no returns of any consequence ; and when some vessels laden with tobacco were consigned to the American commissioners in Paris, Beaumarchais expostulated, but received no explanation. No answer came to any of his letters, nor the slightest sign of recognition from a government in whose cause he was straining every nerve.

The English ambassador in Paris, having got wind of the transaction, had complained of it as an infringement of the treaty between the two countries, and Vergennes felt himself obliged to disavow and discountenance a proceeding which he secretly favored. So vessels were detained in port, and cargoes attached, and the representative of Hortalez & Co. must have had his patience sorely tried as he travelled in hot haste from Havre to Bordeaux, making herculean efforts to collect and despatch his stores in face of countless difficulties. At last, confounded by this persistent non-recognition, he sent an agent to America, M. de Francey, — rather too young a man for the purpose. He came over in the same ship with Baron Steuben and some gallant French officers, whom Beaumarchais and Marie Antoinette had fired with enthusiasm for America. The agent was disgusted with everything, saw nobody to admire but General Washington, and sent to his patron the most dismal and discouraging letters. Lee's friends were powerful, and the cabal had taken into partnership a disaffected sea-captain, named Ducoudray, who had been discharged by Beaumarchais for incompetency, and who now wrote a pamphlet against him, which was published in America, and helped to manufacture prejudice and create an unfavorable public opinion. De Francey did succeed, however, in getting members of Congress to read the correspondence between Beaumarchais and Vergennes. This may have made some impression, for in 1779, after two years and a half of thankless toil, he received at last a letter of acknowledgment in the name of Congress, written by the president, and ending thus : —

> While by your rare talents you were rendering yourself useful to your prince, you have gained the esteem of this new-born republic, and have earned the applause of the New World.
>
> JOHN JAY, *President.*

The enthusiasm of Beaumarchais had remained unabated through all this discouragement. He confidentially writes to his angry, discomfited agent: —

"In spite of all these annoyances, the news from America fills me with joy. Brave, brave people! Their military prowess fully justifies my esteem and the fine enthusiasm felt for them in France. In short, my friend, I look anxiously for returns to enable me to meet my engagements here, mainly that I may then make new arrangements for their advantage."

At last, a direct question from the chairman of a congressional committee brought out the explicit declaration, that the supplies for America, transmitted by Beaumarchais, were not given by the king. The debt was then acknowledged, payment promised, and all would have gone on smoothly but for two unfortunate circumstances. One was that Beaumarchais' accounts, presented in 1788, were referred to a committee of three, of which his arch-enemy, Arthur Lee, was chairman; and the other was that mysterious affair of the "lost million."

In 1776, six months before the signing of the Declaration of Independence, this receipt was signed: —

"I have received from M. Duvergier, conformably to the orders of the Comte de Vergennes, on the 5th instant, the sum of one million livres, *for which I am to account to the aforesaid Comte de Vergennes.*
"CARON DE BEAUMARCHAIS."

The King of France, long after this, loaned and gave large sums to the American commissioners to carry on the war. In 1783 Franklin signed a receipt for nine millions gratuity; yet three years after, on his return to America, it was discovered that only eight millions had passed through the hands of our banker in Paris. Dr. Franklin conjectured that the missing million must have been given to Beaumarchais for our use. In 1794 the government of France was often in unskilled hands, and Gouverneur Morris, then our envoy, contrived to get from the minister of foreign affairs the receipt already quoted as given to Vergennes. Thenceforth Beaumarchais was charged with that sum, and his accounts were persistently disputed, remaining unsettled for fifty years. Talleyrand wrote, exonerating him. The French government exerted itself in his favor, and through its successive ambassadors to this country unwearyingly asserted the justice of his claim; declaring over and over again, officially, that he had accounted for that million to its entire satisfaction; nay, even went so far as to explain and assert that it was given as secret service money, and not meant for supplies, at all. However that may have been, the fact remains that his claims, after being referred to six committees of Congress (three reporting favorably, and three adversely), were set aside till 1835, thirty-six years after the death of Beaumarchais; and a settlement was effected then only by the most persistent importunity on the part of his representatives.

In exile, in 1795, from a garret near Hamburg, he addresses the following letter to the American people: —

"Americans, I have served you with indefatigable zeal. During my life bitterness has been my only reward, and I die your creditor. Permit me, then, as a dying man, to bequeath to you my only daughter, and to endow her with what you owe me. . . . Perhaps Providence has designed, by this delay in your payment, to provide her with means after my death, thus saving my child from utter destitution. Adopt her as a worthy daughter of the state.

"If you refuse this, if I could fear that you would deny justice to myself or my heirs, desperate, ruined, by Europe as well as by you, I should have only one prayer, — for a respite which might allow me to go to America. Arrived amongst you, broken down in mind and body, I should be carried to your capital, to the doors of your national assembly, with my accounts in my hand; and there, holding out to all passers-by the cap of Liberty, with which no man more than myself has helped to adorn your brows, I should cry out: Americans! alms for your friend, for whose accumulated services behold the reward, 'Date obolum Belisario'!"

This man, who, beginning life as a watchmaker's apprentice, had made himself an inventor, a courtier, a teacher in the royal family, a banker, a shipping merchant on a larger scale than the Medici, a dramatic author of the greatest popularity, a diplomatist, a cabinet counsellor, and a master of eloquence of European renown, was also a great publisher. The story of his two editions of Voltaire, complete for the first time, is a chapter by itself. "Haunted by the fear of mediocrity," as he used to say, he bought paper-mills in the Vosges and went to England to purchase the famous Baskerville types, so as to have the best of materials; and when he could find no place for his printing-press in France, on account of prohibition, he persuaded the Margrave of Baden to let him have the dismantled fortress of Kehl for that purpose. As Loménie says, "To superintend the manufacture, printing, and publication of these one hundred and sixty-two volumes, included in two editions of fifteen thousand copies each, and smuggle them into France, really with the connivance of the government, but still at the risk of prohibition, was a laborious enterprise for a man already overwhelmed by the pressure of business." Maurepas had encouraged him to persevere in the work, and had assured him of his sanction; but he died in 1781, and his death was a heavy blow to Beaumarchais. He managed, however, to interest Calonne, the successor of Maurepas, and in three years' time, had completed this great task. It may be mentioned that this is the first time we hear of premiums and a lottery in connection with subscriptions for a book. The notes contributed by the editor are few in number, but characteristic. For instance, where Voltaire writes to M. d'Argental, "An ardent, impetuous, passionate man like Beaumarchais may give a box on the ear to his wife, and possibly two boxes on the ear to his two wives, but he does not poison them," he adds this note: "I certify that this Beaumarchais, sometimes beaten by women, like most men who have loved them too well, never committed the disgraceful act of lifting his hand against one of them."

We have come now to the most brilliant part of his career. The new parliament of Louis XVI., several years before, had triumphantly reinstated him in his civil rights, and had reversed the unfavorable decision in the La Blache case. He was a man of large fortune and great renown, married for the third time to a charming woman, and on familiar terms with those most famous in fashion, politics, and letters. His liberality and kindness seem as inexhaustible as his energy, and his private correspondence and business papers teem with many touching proofs of his sympathy for unfortunate people, who had no claim whatever upon him but their sorrows. He gave not only money but his precious time and the magnetic virtue of his cordial interest. The "Barber of Seville" had acquired the popularity it still maintains, giving him a high place in the fraternity of dramatic authors; but now he produced the "Mariage de Figaro." Probably he had no definite design of disturbance in writing this comedy, which flashed out upon the wrongs of the poor and the abuses of the powerful; but Napoleon said of it, "It is the Revolution in action."

Madame Campan has told us of her reading the manuscript aloud to Marie Antoinette and her husband, and how the king walked up and down the room, when she came to the famous monologue, exclaiming, "This is detestable! It shall never be played. So long as the Bastille stands, the representation of this piece would be a dangerous folly. This man sports with everything that should be respected in a government." "Can't it be played?" urged the queen. "Certainly not," answered Louis XVI. "You may be sure of that." So the representation was forbidden. No one sided with the king but his brother, the Comte de Provence, and M. Mirosmenil, the keeper of the seals. All the fashionable world longed for the forbidden fruit, and ran wild to hear the author read it in private. You heard on all hands, "I am going to-night to hear M. Beaumarchais read the 'Mariage de Figaro';" or, "Are you invited to-morrow to hear the 'Mariage de Figaro'?" The Duc de Fronsac, son of the Duc de Richelieu, writes to the author to entreat him, as a great favor, to read it at the hôtel of the Princesse de Lamballe, and Catherine of Russia sends for him to bring it out in St. Petersburg. The manuscript used at these readings is still extant, tied with faded pink ribbons, and the words "*opuscule comique*" on the outside, in the author's handwriting.

After a three years' battle between Beaumarchais and all Paris, on the one hand, and the king, his brother, and the keeper of the seals, on the other, the popular party gained the day, and the piece was represented. The effect was prodigious. Beaumarchais himself says, "If there is one thing more extravagant than my piece, it is its success."

"It will come to an end," said one of his enemies, behind the scenes, on the evening of the first representation. "Yes," answered Sophie Arnould, "fifty times over." The witty actress was wrong; it was acted more than a hundred times in succession.

The elder brother of the king had been very much annoyed on the opening night, and through a M. Suard constantly sent to the newspapers unfavorable criticisms of the piece and abuse of its author, suggested, if not written by Monsieur himself. Whether Beaumarchais knew this or not, he began by replying with his usual gayety and readiness, but after a while, weary, probably, of the whole thing, he sent a communication to the *Journal de Paris*, declining in future to notice these attacks, and saying that "when he had brought out his play in spite of lions and tigers, he did not mean, after it had succeeded, to spend his time fighting every morning, like a Dutch servant-girl, the vile insect of the night." "Monsieur" took the insult to himself, and went in high dudgeon to the king, whom he found playing cards, and who consented at once to punish this daring Beaumarchais by writing on the seven of clubs, which he held in his hand, an order for his immediate incarceration in the prison of St. Lazare, used as a house of correction for young offenders. The king may have given vent in this way to his suppressed irritation in regard to the piece. It must be said, however, that it is the only act of inexcusable tyranny attributed to Louis XVI.

One roar of laughter went up from Paris the next morning, when it was known that this favorite author and illustrious man was shut up in prison for his impetuous sally. He stayed there only three days, and at last was almost entreated to come out. The king had repented of his precipitation, and may have been rendered uneasy by the popular demonstration, which was losing its jocular tone, and becoming serious in its character. He sent the prisoner a handsome sum of money, which was declined all but a hundred francs, — the amount, perhaps, of his expenditure during his detention. On his release he repaired to the theatre, where the obnoxious play was being represented, and received an uproarious welcome. It was a long time before the actors could go on, and the deafening applause was renewed when they came to this phrase in the great monologue: "Not being able to degrade wit, they maltreat it." Soon after this the "Barber of Seville" was acted at the Trianon, the queen herself taking the part of Rosine; and the author was invited to be present, a delicate way of making reparation for the insult which he had received.

Apart from its historic significance, the "Mariage de Figaro" does not interest us to-day. The plot is objectionable, and the wit often licentious. Most of the abuses he satirizes no longer exist, though we may still need reminding, even here in the United States of America, that "without the privilege of blaming, no praise is flattering," and that "only petty men dread insignificant writings."[1] One passage, however, commonly omitted in representation, though found in all standard editions of the play, may be worth quoting. Marceline, the mother of Figaro, is speaking, and she says, —

"Men, more than ungrateful, who wither with your scorn the playthings of your passions, your victims, you should be made to suffer also for the errors of our youth. . . . What employment is there left for these miserable

---

[1] Il n'y a que les petits hommes qui redoutent les petits écrits.

young women? They have a natural right to busy themselves with female apparel, and thousands of men are set to work upon it."

Figaro, angrily: "Yes, even the soldiers now are made to embroider."

Marceline: "Even in the higher ranks women obtain from you only derisive consideration, lured by pretended respect into real servitude,[1] treated as irresponsible minors in regard to our property, and punished as responsible beings for our faults."

So a reformer of the present day may find a text in the "Mariage de Figaro."

The Parisian public was very much excited at this time by the production of his philosophical, political, and scientific opera, entitled "Tarare," in which he aimed at producing all the effect of a Greek drama, combining dancing, music, and poetry with more solid attractions, but substituting scientific statement for the Greek mythology. The best pupil of Gluck, Salieri, composed the music, and the piece had a great run. Wonderful to relate, it was popular, and kept its place on the stage, under different metamorphoses, till 1819.

The 14th of July, 1789, found Beaumarchais busily superintending the erection of a magnificent dwelling-house, close by the Bastille. He did not occupy it till 1791, and it was thenceforth a fertile source of annoyance in those troublous times. It became the wonder of Paris, but in 1818 it was pulled down, to carry out the new plans for improving the city. Beaumarchais took charge of the demolition of the Bastille at his own request, but he was far from sympathizing with the extremists, and wrote an

[1] Traitées en mineures pour nos biens, punies en majeures pour nos fautes.

address to the French people, which he sent to the Jacobins. It begins thus: "I defy the devil to carry on any business in these frightful days of disorder, misnamed liberty;" and he ends with these words: "O my weeping country, O wretched Frenchmen, to what purpose have you overthrown Bastilles, if robbers are to come and dance over the ruins, and slaughter us upon them? Friends of freedom, know that license and anarchy are its executioners. Join me in demanding laws of these deputies, who owe them to us, who have been made our representatives solely for that purpose. Let us be at peace with Europe. Was it not the most glorious day of our lives when that peace was proclaimed to the world? Your maxims will be established, will be propagated, far better, if you are shown to have been made happy by them, — far better than they can possibly be by war and devastation. Are you happy? Tell the truth. Is it not with French blood that our land is deluged? Speak! is there one of us who has not tears to shed? Peace, laws, and a constitution, — without these blessings we have no country; worse than all, no freedom!" A man who writes, signs, and publishes such words as these on the sixth of March, 1793, and then stays in Paris, is not cowardly. As Sainte-Beuve says: "The only wonder is that he kept his head on his shoulders."

In 1792 France needed arms, and Beaumarchais undertook to obtain them in Holland. Sent after them in 1794 by the committee of public safety, he was put on the list of emigrants by the department of Paris, which confiscated his property, seized and destroyed his papers, imprisoned his sister, wife, and daughter, and declared him a public enemy. He took refuge at last in Hamburg, and could not return till long after the death of Robespierre had opened the prison doors and set his family at liberty. His daughter had a horror of their magnificent house, where they had all suffered so much; nothing could induce her to return to it; so she hid herself away with her mother, while his sister Julia, in order to preserve the property from destruction, lived there entirely alone, in great poverty, for a whole year, subject to constant annoyance from domiciliary visits. At last, under the Directory, they were reunited in the great house, and Beaumarchais tried to gather up what was left of the wreck of his fortune. The old man felt the prevailing enthusiasm for Bonaparte, and addressed some verses to the young conqueror, adjuring him to add one more to his glorious deeds, and remember the prisoners at Olmutz. It was like Beaumarchais to remind him of Lafayette then. He had also become much interested in the use to be made of balloons, in war and in peace, and busied himself in preparing a memorial, addressed to the Directory, on the massacre of the French plenipotentiaries at Rastadt. This was his last work. On a May morning, 1799, the old man was found dead in his bed: probably the cause of his death was apoplexy. The last evening with his family had been gay and pleasant, as usual.

He left an only child, his daughter Eugénie, married, after the Terror, to M. Delarue, aid-de-camp to Lafayette. His widow writes after his death, "Our loss is irreparable: the companion of twenty-five years has vanished, leaving only useless regret, a terrible loneliness, and ineffaceable memories. He readily forgave his enemies, and gladly overlooked an injury. He was a good father, a zealous and serviceable friend, and the born champion of any absent person attacked in his presence. Superior to the petty jealousy so common among men of letters, he counselled and encouraged all, helping them with his money and advice. We should be grateful for the manner of his death; it saved him the pain of parting. He quitted this life as unconsciously as he entered it."

He had been quite deaf for the last few years, but he never lost his enjoyment of a joke, and liked to sign himself, "The first poet in Paris, entering by the Porte St. Antoine." The inscription on the collar of his little dog has often been quoted: "I am Mlle. Follette. Beaumarchais belongs to me. We live on the Boulevard."

Sullied by the faults and vices of his day and generation, dissolute at times in life and utterance, he yet seems to have been invariably generous and affectionate in his family relations, and was idolized as a son and a brother. Fond of display and reckless in speculation, always savoring somewhat of an adventurer, he still devoted himself unremittingly and unsparingly to works of public utility and private beneficence. Imprudent, often quixotic in these enterprises, he was nevertheless remarkable for practical knowledge and shrewd common sense. His energy and industry were wonderful, and his kindness of heart and ready sympathy appear to have been inexhaustible.

His bust stands to-day in the Comédie Française in Paris. Should there not be a niche in American memories for our friend in need; a man like him, thus associated with the early days of our history; one who, while striving to help himself, never forgot to help others? Was not Eugénie Delarue justified in the pride with which she said to the conqueror of Austerlitz, "I am the daughter of Beaumarchais"?

FRENCH WOMEN BEFORE THE REVOLUTION

It was a great misfortune to be born a girl in a noble French family of the eighteenth century; for all the interest centred in the boys, and the daughters were to be disposed of as cheaply as was consistent with their name, consigned to a loveless marriage, or the relaxed rule of convent life. Before Jean Jacques Rosseau shamed mothers into nursing their own children, the poor little creatures were hustled off at once to the country, there to stay with the foster-nurse till old enough to be intrusted to the care of a governess, who occupied, with her charge, some remote part of the house quite out of the way. The children only left this secluded apartment at eleven o'clock, when they were usually taken for a few minutes to their mother's dressing-room to say good-morning, and the little girl was permitted to kiss her mamma, provided she did so politely, under her chin, so as not to rub off the rouge. In pleasant weather, clad in all their best attire, they also walked once a day in the Tuileries garden, but no romping was allowed.

The governess was expected to teach her pupils to read, write, and hold themselves straight. At the age of seven music-lessons began. The little girl had a master for the harpsichord, learned to dance, and was also taught her catechism.

There were children's balls and baptisms, and on both occasions these unfortunate creatures appeared attired in high head-dresses and paniers. They even wore rouge. At the age of eleven or twelve they were usually sent to some fashionable convent. In the delightful book by Lucien Perey, entitled, "The Life of a Great Lady in the Eighteenth Century," we find very interesting descriptions of one of these schools for girls of high rank. Often married between the ages of twelve and fifteen, they sometimes returned to the convent immediately after the ceremony to take up their school life again, and complete their education before assuming the responsibilities of married women, and entering the gay world bearing the name of husbands chosen for them by friends and relatives without any reference to the wishes of the girls, often without any previous acquaintance. This was especially the case when the contracting parties were of high rank.

In the memoirs of Madame d'Epinay we have the following account of the way in which Madame d'Houdetot was married, and we cannot wonder at her subsequent unhappiness.

"M. de Rinville called on M. de Bellegarde to propose one of his cousins, a well-behaved young man, as a. husband for his god-daughter, M. de Bellegarde's daughter Mimi. They appoint a day for a great dinner, to which all the members of both families are invited, and Mimi is made aware of the importance of the occasion.

"Being introduced on her arrival at the de Rinvilles', the Marquise d'Hondetot, mother of the bridegroom elect, kissed all the Bellegardes, root and branch. At dinner, Mimi was placed beside the young d'Houdetot, while the mother took possession of M. de Bellegarde, and by the time they came to the dessert the marriage was openly discussed. When coffee had been brought in, and the servants had retired, 'Well,' said M. de Rinville, 'here we are all together; there is no occasion for so much mystery. What do you say, M. de Bellegarde, yes or no : does my cousin suit you, and does he suit your daughter? Let us come to the point. Our young count is already in love. If your daughter likes him, let her say so. Speak up, my god-daughter.' Mimi blushed very much, but said nothing. One of the ladies present interposed, exclaiming, ' Oh, give them time to breathe!'—'Very well,' said M. de Rinville, 'we can arrange the preliminaries, and leave these young people to talk a little together.' No sooner said than done. The two fathers went into a corner to discuss the dowry and settlements, and in a few minutes rose and came forward, saying, 'It is all decided. We can sign the contract to-night, publish the banns Sunday, and get a dispensation for the rest, so that Monday can be the wedding-day. It will be easy to leave word with the notary and give all the invitations on our way home.'

" That very evening, at the house of M. de Bellegarde, the contract was signed by the members of these two families, till that day almost total strangers to each other. While the notary was reading the agreement aloud, the Marchioness d'Houdetot called Mimi across the room and gave her two caskets of family diamonds, of which the value was left in blank in the contract, there being no time to appraise them. Everybody signed ; they sat down to supper, and the wedding took place on the following

Monday. The night before the wedding all the intimate friends and relations called to inspect the 'corbeille,' given by the bridegroom, and the next day the bride, attired in cloth of silver trimmed with seed-pearls and brilliants, with orange blossoms in her hair, entered the church, escorted by two groomsmen.

"Noon was the common hour for weddings; but the ceremony sometimes took place after midnight. The bride was expected to kiss all the women who were invited, and she presented each one with a fan and hand-bag. Then came the wedding tour that lasted about a week, the newly married couple usually going to some chateau belonging to some of the family.

"On their return they were to appear in state at the opera in an especial box reserved for these occasions. Next came the presentation at court, and the inexperienced girl, launched in society, was henceforward beset by the numberless temptations of the fashionable world at that corrupt period. If she had fallen in love with her husband, and he had felt the charm of her youth and freshness, all went well for a time; but not infrequently wedded life became monotonous, and he soon sighed for his bachelor freedom."

If it was bourgeois to be devoted to your husband, and still more so to expect him to be devoted to you, it was hopelessly ridiculous to be punctilious in attention to religious duties, and few women of rank and fashion personally superintended their households. Naturally there was a great deal of waste and lazy inefficiency; but then high-bred servants never expected to do much work.

Goncourt gives the following description of the life of a fine lady in the eighteenth century: "She opened her eyes about eleven o'clock behind the close-drawn curtains of her bed in the carefully shaded room, and summoned her maid, who lighted the fire and then brought her a cup of chocolate. Sitting on the side of her couch, perhaps playing with a lap-dog, she allowed the attendant to put on her slippers and pass a skirt over her head. Then, after her ablutions, she was rolled in an easy-chair in front of her toilet-table. The door had already opened to admit a gallant who, seated by the great carved chest that holds the dresses, one elbow resting on the toilet-table, watched the proceedings with friendly interest, making a suggestion now and then.

"Then came the 'grand levee,' more visitors arrived,— wits, statesmen, officers of the royal household. Compliments abounded, and all the news was told. Notes were read and answered on a corner of the toilet, while the hair-dresser ignored, and sometimes at his wits' end, endeavored to arrange the fair tresses in the last complicated style. 'If she would only sit still!' Tradesmen sent their goods to be inspected, the Beau Brummels of the day gave their opinion about the becomingness of such a tint or fashion, the doctor called, and the last pamphlet or *bon-mot* was discussed. Once dressed, the lady took her lesson on the harp or harpsichord, or practised the last new song. Perhaps, if she were a patient of Tronchin, the Rousseau of medicine, she might order a horse with gay housings, his mane braided with ribbons, and, followed by a servant, gallop to the Bois de Boulogne, dressed in a green satin jacket braided with gold, and a pink skirt trimmed with silver lace. Sometimes, towards the end of the century,— in 1786, for instance, when they tried hard to be simple,— she wore instead a nankeen riding-habit with ivory buttons, three rolling collars, and a little green vest with a white cravat of flimsy gauze loosely knotted about her throat. The head-gear for this remarkable riding-dress was a canary-colored felt hat with green and white plumes, and the hair tied in a queue hung down the back.

Before the great doctor, Tronchin, had made exercise in the open air fashionable, the reading of the last new tale by Marmontel, or a pamphlet of Beaumarchais, filled up the time till the dinner hour, that varied from one to four o'clock.

"After dinner the carriage came to the door, and the lady made visits, did a little shopping, went to see the last fine piece of tapestry on exhibition, or perhaps to a fire if, fortunately for her, there happened to be a conflagration. Then about sunset she alighted at the entrance of the Tuileries garden, the palace being then unoccupied. This was the fashionable promenade, and parties were sometimes made to sup informally at the gate-keeper's. In the evening, the gate once locked, they could have the garden all to themselves. Or perhaps there was an entertainment at some great house in 'Cours-la-Reine' where the festivities were kept up till dawn. More frequently, however, when it was not an opera night nor an especial occasion at the theatre, the fashionable world congregated in summer-time at some one of the great fairs in and about Paris. Later the boulevards took the place of the Tuileries as a promenade, especially on Thursdays. Towards 1750 a taste for science prevailed, and after dinner, now deferred till three o'clock, the women of fashion went to hear lectures, to see experiments at the Jardin des Plantes, or to Greuze's studio to admire his last picture. The triflers would make up parties to have their profiles cut out in paper, or would sit in their carriages to see the procession of three hundred and thirteen French slaves recently ransomed in Algiers. Sometimes, after paying for a mass to be said for the success of a balloon ascension, they would call on the aerostat and bid him godspeed with a kiss."

In one of the books of this period we find a sketch of the pastimes of a fashionable woman: "As she drives along the boulevard she espies an acquaintance, and, stopping her carriage, invites him to accompany her to her anatomy lesson. On the way they meet a mutual friend, a fair lady, who urges them to give her their advice at an important consultation at her milliner's. On leaving the shop, a servant in livery accosts the lady. He is the bearer of a message from his master, who begs them to go with him to witness some new experiments in gases. 'With all my heart!' the lady answers; 'I should like nothing better. Only you must solemnly promise that there shall be no explosions. How kind of you,' she continues to the Baron, who is now standing by the carriage door. 'Get in with us and tell the coachman where to go.' The Baron gives the address, but before they arrive at the designated place she exclaims, 'But I had entirely forgotten my lesson in physics. Why won't you all come there with me first?' They agree to do so; but on the way a new importation of parrots, at a bird fancier's, catches the lady's eye; she alights, makes some new acquisition, and starts again, recognized, however, by a gentleman, who stops the carriage to say that they must go with him to the Blind Asylum to see the printing. How delightfully unique! but just then some one mentioning a new picture that may be sent away soon, it is decided that, since the printing for the blind will probably go on indefinitely, it is best to go at once to the painter's studio. The conversation takes an artistic turn, and one of the party acknowledging that he paints a little as an amateur, they resolve immediately to stop at his hotel to see his pictures. Before they reach the door, however, the lady cries out, 'Good heavens! I had entirely forgotten that the century-plant in the King's garden is in full bloom to-day. Unless we see it now we never shall have another chance in all our lives.' Whereupon escort number one says to his fair friend, 'But, madame, I thought you were going to your anatomy lesson?'"

Pets of all kinds were numerous,—lap-dogs, great Angora cats, parrots, squirrels, and monkeys, and every little while there was a mania for some new amusement. At one time cutting out pictures to paste on screens was all the rage, and beautiful, rare engravings were destroyed in great numbers in that way. Then jumping-jacks were in vogue, and were ordered at high prices from celebrated painters of the day, Boucher, for instance. In 1749 these toys went out of fashion, and fabulous sums were paid for cups and balls with which every one played. Crochet and netting next came in vogue, and ladies took their work to the theatre. But the greatest craze of all was "parfilage," —unravelling stuffs so as to get the gold and silver threads interwoven; and the wonderful stories told of the money that could be made in this way remind one of the tales we have all heard of the rewards awaiting the indefatigable collector of half a million of postage-stamps. It was hard for a man with braided coat to escape the scissors of these fair spoilers, and it is said that the Duke of Orleans had imitation lace sewed on his court-dress so as to cheat his robber-friends in the salons he frequented.

About midway in the century, with an interval of fifteen months before 1753, — an *interregnum* spent in close confinement at Dijon, — the brilliant châtelaine Louise de Bourbon, granddaughter of the great Condé, held high court at Sceaux, about five miles south of Paris. Born in 1676, she was married, when only sixteen, to the Duke of Maine, son of Louis XIV. and Madame de Montespan. He was the beloved and docile pupil of Madame de Maintenon, a man of literary and scientific tastes, rather inclined to devotion. At the time of their marriage Louise de Bourbon was so tiny and frail that she looked hardly more than ten, but even then she was remarkable for her incessant activity of body and mind.

She is not attractive morally on account of her phenomenal egotism. So long as any one contributed to her comfort, pleasure, or amusement, she was delightful, and seemed very loving; but if the same person on whom she had lavished caresses died, or passed out of her life, she never took the trouble even to affect a grief that she seems incapable of feeling. She was an author of some repute, among other things writing lively comedies, in which she liked to take the principal part at her private theatricals of frequent occurrence.

There was always an apartment at Sceaux kept in readiness for Voltaire, who often produced light plays and proverbs for the stage of the château. It was there, too, that he wrote "Zadig;" and his "Oreste" is dedicated to the Duchesse du Maine.

She had always been a great pet of Louis XIV., and, after his death, terribly disappointed to find her husband and herself overshadowed by the Orleans family, the Duchess conspired against the Regency, and was summarily punished by fifteen months' imprisonment in the castle of Dijon. Her husband, whom she had drawn into the plot, was confined in the citadel of Doullens; and the only companion of this brilliant butterfly, in her close confinement of more than a year, was a waiting-woman in the employ of her enemy, the Duke of Orleans.

Once more restored to liberty, the Duke du Maine did not seem very eager to go back to Sceaux, where his wife, as soon as she was set free, began to reorganize her old court. She had been obliged, however, to take an oath that she would never again interfere in politics; and she kept her word.

For her own amusement the Duchess at once revived an order of chivalry that had been a secret society in her political phase. Both women and men were members; and it was called the "Order of the Bee"—"*L'ordre de la Mouche à Miel.*" Their device, taken from the Aminta of Tasso, once quoted to describe her as a girl, was, "Piccola si, ma fa pur *gravi* le ferite:"—" She is little, but she *does* sting." She herself was the Queen-bee, and on initiation all swore fealty to their sovereign. The oath was as follows: "I solemnly swear, by the bees of Mount Hymettus, fidelity and obedience to the perpetual directress of the order, to wear all my life the medal of the Bees, and, if I prove false to my oath, I hope that for me honey may turn into gall, wax into tallow, and flowers to nettles, and that wasps and hornets may plague me with their stings."

At the ceremony of initiation an immense hive was placed in the middle of a large, green carpet, sprinkled with silver bees. As soon as all had taken their places the top of the hive was lifted so as to form a canopy, under which appeared the grand-master of the order in the guise of an enormous bee. He was seated on a throne, and, as a sceptre, held a dart three feet long. Then the herald came forth, bowed low before the Duchess, and read aloud the statutes of the order, the grand-master threatening with his dart those whose gayety tended to become obstreperous. The festivities ended with dancing around the hive. The dress of the Duchess on these occasions was gorgeous, — a robe of green satin, low-necked, embroidered with silver bees; a crown of emerald bees on her head, and a mantle of cloth of gold fastened to her shoulders. The chevaliers, thirty-nine in number, all wore surcoats of cloth of gold embroidered with silver bees, and each one was decorated with a gold medal, bearing on one side the initials of Louise, Baronne de Sceaux, and on the other a bee buzzing about a hive. The herald was robed in scarlet satin also embroidered with the emblem; and he wore on his head a cap shaped like a beehive. After the revival of the society, when political intrigues were forbidden, the order seems to have resolved itself, at its regular meetings, into what we should now call a "Game Club," the members taking turns in proposing and organizing various diversions.

The splendid château where all these festivities took place, with its rare art-treasures, its portraits and fresco-paintings by Lebrun, was destroyed in 1798. Fortunately a few statues were saved that now adorn the Luxembourg gallery. The great park belongs now to the Duke of Trévise, who has built a new château; but a little corner of this grand estate, formerly the delight of Colbert, has been bought by a company, and its old terraces and shady gardens have been for years a democratic resort, — Les bals de Sceaux.

It has been said that the age of Louis XV. was all for the present, and that of Louis XVI. all for the future.

There is certainly a marked contrast if we turn from the château de Sceaux and its brilliant frivolity to the Parisian salons described in 1765 by Horace Walpole, in his letters to Sir Horace Mann. Hardly more than ten years have elapsed, and what a transformation! Anglomania now prevailed; and the old-bachelor admirer of poor, blind Madame du Deffand complains bitterly of the assiduous devotion to whist and dissertations. "Nothing can be more unvaried," he says, "than the routine in the fashionable world. You dine at half-past two, sup at ten. When you do not go to the theatre, you begin a rubber of whist before supper, leave it in the middle, partake of three courses and a dessert, and then go back to the card-table, where there is often a second rubber. Then the women bring out their crochet, you draw up your chairs, and an interminable discussion begins of some literary or religious question till it is time to go to bed, or, more properly speaking, time to get up." The rage for whist and Clarissa Harlowe seemed to him equally absurd, and he was disgusted with the popularity of Hume, just then the great social success.

It is interesting to read his observations upon the place accorded to women in French society, so different from their position in England where, he says, men treat women with no more respect than their horses.

Horace Walpole's cousin, wife of the English ambassador in Paris, tells him that between the ages of thirty and forty women are much more admired in France than when they were very young, and he decides that she is right. Quite carried away by their charm, he exclaims, "If you should ask me who are the really agreeable people of my acquaintance, I should answer, 'A great many Frenchwomen, some Englishmen, a few Englishwomen, and *very few Frenchmen.*'" In fact, he does not like the men at all, though he is very happy in Paris when he has successfully asserted his right to do as he pleases, never to touch a card, nor to take part in an argument. He obtains even a dispensation from doing homage to the authors who are lionized in the "salons." "Every woman of fashion," he writes, " has two or three of these plants, and, Heaven knows, they are well watered."

How many interesting women are sketched by him in his portrait-gallery letters!

The two great salons at this time were really two rival courts, the only ones in Paris, since the King lived eight miles away at Versailles. One of these salons was at the Palais Royal and the other at the Temple.

The Orleans family, of course, reigned at the Palais Royal; and their court was presided over by the beautiful Madame de Blot, lady in waiting to the Duchesse de Chartres. As good as she was beautiful, she had converted the Duke of Orleans from a passionate admirer into a most respectful and devoted friend.

After reading Clarissa Harlowe, however, Madame de Blot becomes a trifle too sentimental for the taste of the nineteenth century. She used to wear around her neck a miniature copy of the façade of the church in which her brother was buried. Another attraction at the Palais Royal seems to have been a lively little fright of a woman, mother-in-law of Marie Antoinette's friend, the Countess Jules de Polignac. One day when some one was praised before her on account of her vivacity, she demurred and said, "Yes, — but her liveliness always suggests fleas."

Then there was the beautiful Marquise de Fleury, with her impulsive, childish ways. We do not wonder that Horace Walpole exclaimed, "How do they manage to get along with her at home?" when we read that one evening, coming back from a court reception at Versailles that she had probably found tiresome, she stopped on her way home at Madame Guémenée's who was receiving, pulled off her trained gown and paniers, and went about among the guests in corset, boa, and a little dimity petticoat, outside of which dangled two large pockets. She had great pride of birth. When Turgot attacked the privileges of the nobles it excited her ire, and she said to a lady who admired him, "However great my respect for the king, I never consider myself indebted to his majesty; nobles have sometimes conferred the royal prerogative on their sovereigns, but I defy you to name any king to whom we owe our rank."

The rival salon at the Temple was the hôtel of the Prince de Conti, where the great attractions were music, sometimes performed by Mozart himself, no ceremony and no servants. At the afternoon teas, noble ladies in fancy dress cut the cake, made and passed around the tea, and at the informal suppers, dumb waiters obviated the necessity of menial service.

Here the observed of all observers was the Countess de Boufflers, so admired by Horace Walpole, always surrounded by women as well as men, who did homage to her unrivalled charm, supreme in spite of her forty years. The Countess Amélie de Boufflers, her daughter-in-law, was always there, a gay and pretty woman, very accomplished and ready at repartee. She could say charming things on the spur of the moment. There was a fashionable game, played a great deal at that time, called "Boats." You were to imagine yourself on the point of perishing, with the two persons whom you loved or ought to love the best, and you were asked the very trying question: If you could only save one, which should it be? The Countess Amelia was supposed to be in the boat with her mother-in-law and her own mother, who had not brought her up, and whom she had scarcely ever seen. When asked which one she should save, she answered, "I should save my mother, and then drown myself with my mother-in-law." She had a very sweet voice, and her harp was a great delight at the chamber concerts, frequently presided over by the Prince de Conti as manager.

All the Court attended the Monday suppers at the Temple, and it shows how small the "beau monde" then was when we read of there being a hundred and fifty persons at once in the Conti drawing-rooms, evidently considered a large assembly by the narrator.

The Condé family gave two great balls in a year, but usually they entertained their guests at Chantilly, where everything was sumptuous and magnificent.

In 1750 the Maréchale de Luxembourg had the most celebrated salon in Paris. She gave usually two suppers a week, and to be received at her house was a criterion of good standing, while to be condemned by her closed every door against you. It was the headquarters of refined society, the school par excellence of good manners.

The Beauvais Hôtel had a peculiar charm in the sympathy and respect inspired by the admirable old couple who gave to the world such a beautiful example of conjugal devotion and faithful attachment to friends through good and evil report. Choiseul in disgrace, Necker in his fluctuating popularity, even Loménie de Brienne in his downfall, found them always the same, sincere, stanch, and true.

The Maréchale d'Anville also kept open house, from which she was apt to be absent when she and Mademoiselle de l'Espinasse had hurried through their dinner so as to go off together to a "séance" at the Academy. A great friend of the Encyclopedists, she obtained a safe conduct for Voltaire when he was in real danger, and was more devoted than any other woman of rank to Turgot and his reforms, her reward being a vulgar popular caricature, in which her name was associated with that of the great minister of finance. She was never cured, however, of her passion for the public good; her heart went out to all utopian schemes, and she sympathized warmly with the most progressive ideas.

In sharp contrast, the Princess de Robecq was a bitter enemy of the Encyclopedists. Under her eye, and in part at her dictation, Palissot wrote his abusive comedy "Philosophes," and, just before her death, she contrived to obtain from the Duke de Choiseul, then minister, permission to have it represented, favorable though he was to the men attacked by Palissot, who apparently aspired to be the French Aristophanes.

Madame du Deffand, who in her fourteen years' correspondence with Horace Walpole gives us such admirable portraits of her contemporaries, is herself an interesting figure. She embodies the dissatisfaction with life and the restless need of amusement, the oppression that seems to weigh down so many persons at that time in the stillness before the storm. Her "herculean weakness," as she calls it, sustains her, blind and old as she is, in the most wearisome round of gayety. M. Caro says that her fear of solitude, and her intimate conviction of the nothingness of the society in which she incessantly sought diversion, illustrates Pascal's saying, "We only seek conversation and amusement because we cannot stay at home alone and enjoy ourselves." It might be said of her, as Chateaubriand once said of himself, that she yawned out her life. Her capacity for friendship is shown when she writes of the President de Hénault, with whom she had been long intimate: "The President is not well. I do not believe he will live through the winter. His loss would be a grief to me, and would make a change in my life." And she says of Mlle, Lespinasse who had been devoted to her during ten years before the great rupture and subsequent rivalry, " Mlle. Lespinasse died last night at two o'clock. Formerly that would have been an event for me; now it is nothing at all."

She never seemed to care truly for any one but Walpole, and this half-posthumous affection makes you smile even while you are sorry for the poor old woman so desperate about this skittish old bachelor. M. Caro, in his admirable sketch, speaks of the passion that forgets how late it is — all the charms of heart and mind lavished by the fascinating woman of seventy-one on the halfscared Hippolytus who seems not to be so much afraid of Phèdre's love as of the ridicule to which she might subject him at his club in London or in the court circle. It is a little psychological episode that excites your sympathy while it provokes a smile.

Correspondence in those days was an engrossing occupation and a fine art. Madame Geoffrin made it a rule never to let a day pass without writing at least two letters, and Madame du Deffand always made two drafts of the most ordinary note or letter.

It is easy to imagine how the health of the French women of the upper classes must have suffered from the artificial life they led. The use of rouge and powder was most injurious, and the unnatural constraint of their dress prevented their deriving any real benefit from what time they spent in the open air. Their head-gear was exceedingly cumbrous, and so complicated that they could not run the risk of disarranging it often by wearing hats, and the close-cut *charmilles* in the gardens and parks were invented to allow them to walk without exposure to the rays of the sun.

Love of nature seems to have been unknown till it was revealed to them by Rousseau; and residence in the country was generally considered tantamount to exile.

In the bourgeoisie life was essentially different. The daughters usually remained under the mothers' direction, except for a year or two passed at a quiet convent, very different from those chosen by the aristocracy.

Akin to the people by the habit of labor, and affiliated with the nobility by opulence, the young girl of the middle class was trained for household duties as well as social obligations. Her life had two sides, one of study and tasteful accomplishments, the other of active occupation, manual labor, or the intelligent superintendence of servants' work. At home one master followed another in the course of the day: teachers of geography, history, music, and drawing, with a dancing-master who taught her to make a low courtesy and other details of graceful demeanor. But these lessons, like the beautiful dresses worn on great occasions, enriched and adorned, but did not constitute her life.

The young daughter interrupted her practising to run out and buy parsley or salad for the table, to go in the kitchen and make an omelet, to shell pease, or to skim the soup. Goncourt says that they seem to have been brought up with the good sense of Molière and the graces of Madame de Pompadour. Marriages were founded on preference; and the young girls were left free to accept or refuse an offer. Sometimes a young man was kept a long time on probation. Though, towards the end of the century they imitated the court fashions in dress and language, their pleasures remained much more healthful and invigorating, excursions in the country, visits to exhibitions of pictures, concerts and theatrical entertainments, such joys as gladdened the girl-life of Mademoiselle Phlipon, for we cannot forget that from this stock came Madame Roland and Charlotte Corday.

Madame de Staël, with her Protestant-Swiss antecedents and education, was an exceptional case of development.

Marie Antoinette, too, was not a product of this eighteenth century civilization, though she was modified by its influences. Only fifteen when she arrived in France, she had led a comparatively unconstrained life, and her education had been sadly neglected, her imperial mother being too much engrossed by state affairs to watch over her little girl's development. Unfortunately the young princess had no taste for reading, nor any idea that such an occupation could be desirable. This incapacity for amusing herself alone proved particularly unfortunate, making her dependent on others, and intensifying her girlish longing for friendships and intimacies often perilous in high places. She was quick to understand and ready at repartee, but deficient in judgment, a defect that had never been corrected. Lovely, gay, and innocently fond of fun, she had a kind heart and a sincere desire to oblige those who needed her help. She was particularly intimate with the Countess de Polignac and her set, and this exclusiveness was unfortunate in a court. Her ideal of happiness seems to have been a round of rural pleasures, simple, but very costly, like those she indulged in at the Trianon; and she excited the resentment of the many who were not included in these parties. Some of the young men of the Polignac circle were among the first to speak jeeringly of the young queen when she chanced to offend them by haughtily repelling undue familiarity too frequently tolerated in that fast set. It has been said that the king's brother, the Count d'Artois, afterwards Charles X., wrote an indecent couplet about her that had a wide circulation. She often committed imprudences. For instance, the Prince de Ligne, father-in-law of Hélène Massalska, tells of the way she used to leave intentionally her lady in waiting far behind in her horseback rides with him in the Bois de Boulogne.

Of course this excited resentment, but the Prince de Ligne says emphatically that what was condemned as coquetry and undue love of admiration was only a hunger and thirst for friendly converse. Two men were especially favored by her, the staid and sedate Duc de Coigny and the young Swede, Fersen, her coachman in the flight to Varennes. Every one knows how attractive she was in appearance, with her beautifully poised head, her noble and graceful bearing, her brilliant complexion, and winning smile. Her feet and hands were also very beautiful, and the fresh, simple dresses of lawn and muslin that she made the fashion seemed peculiarly suited to her radiant loveliness. She could be very queenly, and in her sorrows showed heroic courage ; but Maria Theresa's imperial mood was not habitual with her. Sainte-Beuve quotes a speech she made, when as Dauphiness she heard a lady blamed for interceding with the shameless Du Barry to save her son's life. Marie Antoinette exclaimed, " It is just what I should have done in her place. If necessary, I could even have thrown myself at the feet of Gamore, the little negro page of the miserable favorite." And long afterwards she showed her mother's heart by refusing to escape from the Temple if her children must be left behind.

Any one who had the great good-fortune to be present at the first representation of " Parsifal " at Bayreuth, with Wagner himself as stage manager, must vividly remember the scene of the flower enchantment, that marvellous garden teeming with tropical vegetation, where houris, in the guise of flowers, wove themselves in living garlands about the hero who repulses them, and how when he at last triumphs over the supreme seduction the magic towers melt away, and a cold November wind whirls about in the dusty gloom great, brown withered leaves that flutter and fall to the ground, all that is left of those fair flowers.

So the gay pageant of the eighteenth century in France vanishes in darkness and horror. That is the first impression as you lose sight of those gay triflers who made the early life of Marie Antoinette a restless round of aimless frivolity, and who overruled the instinctive determination of Louis XVI. that the " Figaro " of Beaumarchais should not be represented.

But, as at Bayreuth the everlasting hills stood out changeless against the background of the sky, pure and blue, so may we not feel that in toil and storm to France was confided the custody of the Holy Grail, the precious recognition of human brotherhood, of a common humanity uplifted then to abide with us once more and forever?

"THE MARVELS OF MONT SAINT MICHEL"

On the coast of Normandy, between Granville and Saint Malo, a mighty mass of granite rock, almost pyramidal in shape, rises abruptly from the level sands that are covered by the sea at high tide. This rock was originally called "Mont Tombe," or Tomb Mountain, from its resemblance to a tumulus. Tradition says, that in the year of our Lord 709, Aubert, a holy bishop of Avranches, a town not far off, had a vision commanding him to build a watch-tower on the top of Mount Tombe for the heavenly sentinel, Saint Michael, to guard the coast, and warn sailors of the peril of the sea. He was told that he would find as a sign on the top of the mount, tied among the bushes, a young bull that had been stolen and hidden there; that he was to return him to his rightful owner, and then to build a chapel large enough to cover all the ground trampled by the animal's feet. He at once repaired to the mount, followed by his workmen, a multitude of peasants singing psalms and hymns. On their arrival they found the bull as they had been told; but on the spot where they were directed to build, two enormous perpendicular stones were embedded. They tried in vain to dislodge them, and were beginning to lose heart, when twelve more men were seen climbing the steep crags.

It was Bain, a vassal of the good bishop, who had come to his help with his eleven stalwart sons. They worked anew with might and main, but the rock stood firm in spite of their efforts. Then the bishop called Bain and said to him, "Have you no other child?" "Yes; there is one left at home." "Why did you not bring him also?" "He was asleep in his cradle." "Go and get him," said the good bishop. When Bain came back with his child, the bishop took the little one in his arms, and pressed his tiny left foot softly on the great rocks, that immediately became loose, toppled over, and fell crashing to the ground below, where, it is said, a fragment can still be seen, bearing the impress of the baby's foot. So the chapel was built, and the bishop established twelve priests in a house adjoining, to praise God night and day, and he endowed the convent with broad lands inherited from his father.

During the ravages of the Northmen, after the death of Charlemagne, the monks wore coats of mail, and drove the pirates away. From that time dates the village, with its houses like swallows' nests, clinging to the craggy rock or niched into the clefts at the base of the mount. In the old chronicles it is called "Pendula Villa," or Hanging-town.

Charles the Simple gave his daughter Gisela in marriage to the Norman Rollo, and Mont Saint Michel was part of her dower. Fortunately the Christian princess converted her rude husband, and he protected the convent and enriched it with his spoils. So the soldier-monks became rich lords, and grew more and more negligent of their religious duties, till, in the time of the third duke, Richard, their conduct was a great scandal. With the consent of Lothaire, the king, Duke Richard turned them out, and gave their places to thirty Benedictine monks from the great Abbey of Jumièges. This was in 966, more than two hundred and fifty years after the foundation of Saint Aubert.

Norgod, the Dane, Bishop of Avranches, had a great affection for the new abbot of Saint Michel, who was a holy man and a great builder, and they often met at low tide on the sands for friendly converse. One night, when the tide was high, and no one could get to the mount, the bishop, before going to sleep, looked from his window towards the monastery, and saw it wrapped in flames. Calling his canons, they passed the night sorrowing in prayer for the dead; but, when the morning broke, the abbey stood untouched and fair in the sunshine and the bewildered bishop met his friend by appointment, as usual, on the sands beneath. That unearthly light has never been seen again; but in modern times, when the holy pile was used as a prison, we are told that strains of celestial music were sometimes heard at night issuing from the deserted, empty church.

In one of Uhland's ballads, he tells a pretty legend of "Mont Saint Michel:" how a poor mother, in pains of childbirth, was left behind in a precipitate flight of pilgrims before the swiftly rising tide, and how, when the tide went out, she was found safe, with her baby smiling on her arm, having been saved from the "cruel, crawling foam" by the miraculous interposition of the Virgin Mary, who had held them from harm in her veil. A curious, cylindrical column, a hundred feet high, erected with great difficulty on the shifting sands, commemorated this miracle, and withstood the action of the waves till the middle of the 17th century, when it was washed away.

There is another legend of a powerful, wicked baron, who laid waste and harried the abbey-lands. The abbot, instead of asking secular aid and driving him off by force of arms, instituted a service called "The Clamor," in which every day after mass he and all his monks, with "*Miserere* and *Kyrie Eleison*," appealed to heaven and asked for deliverance from this bad man. The baron knew of the "Clamor" from popular report, and at first seemed to care nothing about it; but, as time went on, he grew exasperated, and one day rode out, at the head of his train, crossed the sands at low tide in military array, and sounded his horn under the walls. When the abbot, an unarmed old man, presented himself in answer to the summons, the baron shouted, "Monk, is it true that you are so bold as to call down, every day, woe on me and mine?" "Yes," calmly answered the holy man; "and I shall continue to do so as long as you wickedly despoil my master and my patron, Saint Michael." Whether the baron saw the saint in person standing by his faithful servant, we are not told, but, falling on his knees, he cried, "Let me be henceforward your soldier!" and, dismounting, received with all his followers the abbot's forgiveness and blessing.

In the "Song of Roland," chanted at the battle of Hastings, we read of the fearful convulsions of nature, of the midnight darkness at noonday, and the shock felt from "Saint Michael's of the Mount to the fair Shrine of Cologne," when Roland died. Taillefer, who rushed into the conflict, singing "of Charlemagne and Roland and Oliver, and the brave barons who fell at Roncevaux," was in the knightly train of the Norman Baron Mortain, who bore the banner of "Saint Michael of the Mount" on that memorable day.

William the Conqueror and his sons were benefactors of the "Mount." Henry II. of England despoiled the community, but made ample restitution at the entreaty of his mother and his wife, and he was several times entertained at the abbey. Once he came accompanied by Thomas à Becket, to meet Louis VII., to arrange the marriage of his son with Marguerite of France, and then he left the Mount afterwards on his way to Avranches to do penance for the murder of the Archbishop.

After the assassination of little Arthur of Brittany by his uncle, Philip Augustus summoned John as his vassal to appear and answer for the crime, and when the recreant King of England failed to do so, the French sovereign declared Normandy forfeit to the crown. From this time, Mont Saint Michel belonged once more to France. In the war that ensued the abbey was burned, taking fire from the conflagration of the village at the base; but it was rebuilt by Philip Augustus at his own expense in joyous celebration of the acquisition, and to his munificence and the architectural genius of several abbots we owe the most magnificent "ex-voto" in the world, the "granite jewel" known as "La Merveille." This appendage to the shrine-fortress of Saint Michel consists of a marvellous structure three stories high, suspended in mid-air. The lower part, called the "Montgomeries," contains the cellars and hall of alms. In the second we see the Hall of the Knights, sometimes called the Hall of Pillars, while the whole is crowned by the cloisters, in which triple rows of slender columns are arranged with such skill that, starting from the angles of two squares of different dimensions, every pillar of the largest quadrangle comes in the centre of the arch of the smallest. The perspective groups them in threes, and the vaulted roof is a series of triangles. The pillars of the colonnade against the walls are of granite, but the others are of various stones of different colors. The church, still higher, is built on a platform, of which the middle rests on the outer verge of the rock. The rest is supported by battalions of massive pillars and solid walls of masonry. The triforium is especially admired. Overhead a chime of nine bells in a lofty tower joyously pealed out, or tolled this invocation:—

> "Thou, who watchest o'er the flow
> Of the waters to and fro,
> In the hollow of thy hand
> Keep thy Pilgrims, as they go
> To the Shrine across the sand."

On the topmost pinnacle stood a large silver-gilt statue of St. Michael mounted on a pyramidal pedestal. It could be seen from a great distance at sea.

Mont Saint Michel has withstood many sieges. One of the most famous is that of Lord Scales, who invested the place for Henry V. He built a series of ports around the walls, and his enormous guns carried stone balls a hundred and sixty pounds in weight. Having made a breach with this formidable artillery, the Englishmen rushed forward to take the fortress by assault, but encountered a wall of steel that withstood the fierce onset. They were twenty to one, but numbers availed little in so small a space. They were repulsed with great loss, pursued and driven back to their forts. When they raised the siege soon after, two of their great guns were captured, and are still shown as trophies at the entrance of the abbey.

During the religious war, after the massacre of "Saint Bartholomew," the Huguenots were determined to get possession of Mont Saint Michel. On the 22d of July, 1579, almost all the villagers and monks had gone to a chapel at Ardevon to keep the feast of Mary Magdalen. They left in procession at daybreak, and at seven in the morning the porters unsuspectingly admitted a party of pilgrims, who seemed to have come from a distance, and who were brought across the sands by the regular guides. They laid aside their arms, as was customary, at the entrance, and after breakfasting at the hostlery, ordered and paid for a high mass, at which they assisted with great apparent devotion. When it was over, they asked to see the relics and curiosities, and while these were being shown, all of a sudden a voice rang out, crying, "Strike! Kill, kill!" Whereupon, these pretended pilgrims, who were really Huguenots in disguise, produced concealed pistols, drew knives from their sleeves, slew the priest at the altar, and attacked the dismayed monks. The sanctuary and courts were full of smoke, and resounded with shouts, cries, and groans. Three of the Huguenots ran out on the ramparts and waved scarfs, a concerted signal for their friends outside. But those villagers who had not gone to Ardevon had heard the uproar, and now saw the strange pilgrims signalling to a troop of horsemen coming full gallop towards the mount. They instantly closed and barred the inner gate between them and the abbey, raised the drawbridge, let the portcullis fall, manned the walls, and prepared to resist. The false pilgrims could not get out, their friends could not get in, and, to make matters worse for the assailants, another band of mounted men came in sight, riding hard, and bearing the banner of a valiant captain, Louis La Moricière, a well-known friend of the "Mount." The Huguenot horsemen fled, and their friends, entrapped, sued for mercy. This was granted, though the men who slew the priest were afterwards executed, and some, fleeing through the intricate passages, met a violent death at the hands of those whom they had so treacherously assaulted. This story is sometimes called "The taking and re-taking of Mont Saint Michel;" but the fortress was never really captured.

La Moricière was now appointed governor, and two of the well-known Huguenot family of Montgomery, learning that he was to be absent for a few days from his post, planned a new attack. Early one morning a cavalcade was seen crossing the sands, ladies richly dressed, apparently of high rank, mounted on pillions behind servants and guided by four fishermen. They appeared harmless enough; but, in truth, all — ladies, servants, and fishermen — were Huguenots armed to the teeth. One who acted as major-domo came forward, and lifting his hat, said to the guard at the gate, "It is Mademoiselle de Saint Auviers, who has come to claim the protection of the dame La Moricière in the present unsettled state of the country." While the man was speaking, one of the pretended maids slipped past the guard inside the gate. A soldier of the garrison chucked her under the chin; but as he did so, cried out, "A beard, a beard!" The beard belonged to a Scotchman, who forthwith planted his dagger in the breast of the soldier; there was a general rush and *mêlée;* the garrison, taken by surprise, made a feeble resistance, and the masqueraders entered the place, leaving the two leaders, in women's clothes, behind to keep the outer gate till the elder Montgomery should arrive. He was already at hand with his light horse and cross-bowmen; but before they came up, one brave citizen encouraged the towns-people to resist, crying, "Don't you see they are only women?"

They bore the leaders back and began to lower the portcullis; but, before it touched the ground, one of the two Huguenots succeeded in driving a ladder underneath. Through this narrow opening the men at arms crawled, the town was sacked and given up to pillage for a week. Meantime La Moricière hurried back with a troop he had raised himself; but they warned him that if he attacked the fortress his wife and children, who were in the town, should pay the penalty. He now bethought him also of a stratagem. Having inhabited the abbey, he knew that in a tower of "La Merveille," adjoining the chapel of Saint Aubert, there was an arrangement of wheels and pulleys used in lifting heavy provisions and articles for the use of the community. To gain access to this tower, he took possession one evening of the chapel, much to the delight of the Huguenots, who promised themselves to unearth him in the morning. But, during the night, the governor succeeded in opening communication with those above, when he and all his men were safely transferred by the pulleys to the interior of the fortress. Before daybreak they made a sudden sortie and rushed through the opened gate and down the steps into the town. The surprise was complete; there was hardly time to call to arms before the steep street ran red with blood. The Montgomeries threw up barricades and fought bravely, but they were obliged to yield, and capitulated under the outer portal with the honors of war. The masquerading captains, however, narrowly escaped with their lives. In memory of this occupation of the village for a week, the Montgomeries had three scallop shells of Saint Michael added to their coat of arms. The pulleys of "La Merveille" and the sortie of La Moricière figure largely in the pictorial representations of that time.

The next year Louis La Moricière was killed at the siege of the neighboring town of Pontorson and a new governor was appointed for the "Mount," whereupon the Montgomeries contrived another plan to get possession of the fortress. For this purpose Gabriel de Montgomery made the acquaintance of a reckless, unprincipled soldier of fortune who promised for a large reward to enlist in the garrison and then to man the wheel and draw up him and his soldiers into the stronghold. After a time the man carried out the first part of his plan and entered the service of the governor; but immediately, whether from sudden remorse or expectation of a double reward, he confessed the whole scheme. The governor ordered him to go on and do exactly as he had promised. Every arrangement at last being complete on both sides, the wretched creature gave the concerted signal, and more than two hundred men crossed the sands unmolested, unperceived as they thought owing to a thick fog, and concealed themselves in the neighborhood of the pulley-tower. Gabriel de Montgomery was on hand, as gay as if bound on a party of pleasure. The traitor, too, was at his post, and at night the cable slowly descended. The boldest of the Huguenot band made himself fast to the rope, gave the signal, mounted, and disappeared in the yawning darkness. All was silence, but for the creaking as the cable wound and unwound. Sixty-eight men were drawn up, but still not a sound was heard. The leaders grew apprehensive, seeing by the thinned ranks that their own turn must soon come. They called anxiously to the man at the wheel, who answered, "All is well." "Throw me down a monk then," said Montgomery; "there are enough of you up there to begin to go to work;" and presently a rigid form in frock and cowl fell at his feet. He could not tell in the darkness that it was one of his own men who lay there dead; but in vague alarm he called out again: "Before I go up I must speak to Rablotière," designating one of his favorite soldiers, who had been among the first to ascend. It happened that the man in question was well known also to the governor, who had spared his life. He was now brought back to the mouth of the well, and the governor promised to make his fortune if he would only reassure his leader. But Rablotière was a brave man, and when Montgomery called out: "What is the matter?" he shouted down, "Treason! Treason!" Whereupon they who were left below lost no time in making the best of their way back to Pontorson. All the soldiers drawn up had been gagged and killed one by one; but it is a relief to know that the governor spared the life of the brave Rablotière. From this fearful slaughter the cellars of "La Merveille" acquired the name of the "Montgomeries."

The abbey came out of the wars with crumbling walls and dilapidated piety. The military had so long superseded the religious rule, that little devotion was left, and the services, mostly performed by hirelings, were spiritless and irregular. The few monks who remained gave themselves up to feasting and dissipation, leading lives that would have disgraced even laymen in that age. Henri de Lorraine de Guise, a child five years old, was made abbot of Mont Saint Michel by the Pope, Paul V.

During the reign of Louis XIV. the abbey occasionally received political prisoners, such as the kidnapped American Patriarch, Avedik, or the wretched pamphleteer, Dubourg, who died here miserably in an iron cage.

In 1793 the monks all fled, and the abbey was pillaged. It would have been given to the flames as well, but for the devotion of a band of volunteers from Avranches, who stood guard night and day, and saved the grand old pile. Under the empire it was used as a prison and penitentiary; but in 1863 the convicts were sent elsewhere, and the bishop of Coutances received permission to restore religious worship in the desecrated shrine. He established there a Brotherhood of Missionary Fathers, who have ever since occupied the convent buildings, and who keep up the daily service; but the entire property is owned and controlled by the government. Under these auspices for some time a judicious restoration has been going on.

Formerly, as has been said, all visitors were obliged to cross the sands on foot, guides were needed on account of the dangerous and shifting quicksands, and only at low tide could they reach the "mount;" but of late years a long dike has been built, access is always possible, and poetical peril has given way to prosaic safety. At the spring-tides, however, there is still a chance for a spice of adventure, and guides are occasionally once more in demand to carry travellers through the waves on their shoulders. The new facility of approach brings tourists as well as pilgrims every year in great numbers; but there is a well-grounded fear expressed lest the washing of the waves, caused by the dike acting as a dam, may sap these venerable walls. The archæologists on one side, and the promoters of travel and pilgrimage on the other, have argued their cause before the Chamber of Deputies; but the dike still remains.

Leaving the railway at Avranches or Pontorson, you can take a wagon for "Mont Saint Michel." The first sight of the pinnacled, church-crowned, fortress-girdled rock, at a great distance across the level plain, is very imposing, and you see how wise the architects were not to lose one foot of such a grand pedestal.

Entering by the gateway, guarded by the captured guns of Henry the V., you find yourself in the single, steep street of the old town at the base, alive at evening with the fishing population in their picturesque habiliments, while white coiffed Sisters of Charity pass silently along with their little orphan charges. The roofs are venerable with mosses and lichens, so that you can hardly tell the houses sometimes from the rock of which they seem to form a part, and as you pass under ruined gateways, and mount grass-grown steps, once trodden by Saint Louis and Duguesclin, the dike is forgotten, the nineteenth century seems far away, and you are deep in the "Middle Ages."

On entering the inn, a clear fire is blazing close to the doorway on the left, lighting up all the bright saucepans and other belongings of the picturesque interior. There is a long, well-garnished spit revolving on the clean-swept hearth, carefully tended by our host in person, in white cap and apron. His wife, the pearl of landladies, now makes her appearance, capable, neat, pretty, and graceful, with an eye to everything, and a courteous word for everybody, as she flits back and forth from her husband at the fire to her guests in the dining-room opposite. You ask to be shown your rooms, and they are pointed out by the charming hostess, who, leading you outside the door, shows you the sign of the establishment high on the perpendicular rock above your head, so high indeed that you are fain to adjourn the ascent till you can make it once for all after dinner.

The evening walk on the ramparts, looking off at the star-lit sea, the glimpse of the community at prayers through the open portal of the old church, only illuminated by the lights in the choir where the dark-stoled figures are gathering in the gloom, the early morning service to which we were summoned by the convent bell, the long exploration, it is all delightful to remember, but hard to describe.

As you mount from the vast crypts, with their massive pillars, to the wonders of the upper air, the forest of finials and the fairy lightness of the "*escalier de dentelle,*" and look down at the hoary walls, where the seabirds build their nests, and up at the towers, waving from every nook and cranny with banners of graceful grasses, and pennons of gay wild flowers, it seems as if Titans must have co-operated with winged workmen to produce the wonderful whole. It is all indescribably beautiful, the interest deepens as you linger, "The knapsack of custom falls off your back," and the American tourist becomes in spirit a devout pilgrim at the ancient shrine of "Mont Saint Michel."

PROVENÇAL SONG

Dance, and Provençal song, and sunburnt mirth. — KEATS.

TRUE it is that this one delicious line from the "Ode to a Nightingale" preserves for us the haunting music of that mediæval strain which seven centuries have not made dull. The very name of Provence brings back those May days when the *châtelaine*, the lady of the castle, having just plucked the first violet in her airy garden, saw with delight the *trouvère* or *troubadour*, with harp or lute slung across his shoulders, toiling up the steep ascent to the rock fortress whence some sparrow-hawk of a baron sallied forth to pounce upon travellers, pillaging and protecting the neighborhood by turns. On the evening of his arrival perhaps all the household — knights, squires, pages, ladies, pilgrims, and men-at-arms — gathered eagerly about him, in the paved court of the castle, to hear him chant his programme, or recite the new lay he had been brooding over all winter long in his humble home.

For the young poet was often of low degree. Peire Vidal was the son of a leather-dresser, and the father of Bernard de Ventadour was a baker. His mother used to bring the wood to heat the ovens, and yet his impassioned songs found favor with Eleanor of Guienne, wife of Louis

VII. of France, and his poetical devotion followed her to England after her marriage with Henry II. Though the subject of the poem was frequently taken from the castle chronicle, the *châtelaine* herself was constantly the object of the troubadour's homage and somewhat conventional adulation. Quinet calls these lyrics "the epithalamium of the nobility and the people," and shows how the necessity of mystifying the expression of their feelings may account for the involved complexity of some of their love poems.

It is true that not all the husbands were like the Lord of Roussillon, in the story of William de Cabestaing, who gave his wife her lover's heart to eat. Some seem to have befriended the gallant, and to have enjoyed the reflected celebrity of his poetical homage. Peire Vidal of Toulouse, the Don Quixote of troubadours, "the craziest man that ever was," says the chronicler, had an intimate friend, a certain Lord Barral. They called each other by the same name, "Raynier," and the troubadour was constantly at the castle. There he paid his court to his friend's wife, the beautiful Azalaïs, to her great annoyance, and her husband's infinite amusement; for one of Peire Vidal's peculiarities was, that he regularly fell in love with every fair lady he saw. He, moreover, believed that they all returned his affection, though in truth they made a great deal of fun of him. One morning early he saw Barral leave his room, and the door was ajar. Then he stole in, knelt down by the bed, and kissed the lady Azalaïs, who was lying there fast asleep. She looked up laughing, thinking it was her husband; but when she saw Peire Vidal instead, she made such an outcry and uproar that all her ladies came running in, and

Peire Vidal escaped. The fair Azalaïs sent at once for her husband, and, bitterly weeping, demanded vengeance. "But Lord Barral," says the chronicler, "like a wise and valiant man as he was, took it as a joke, and laughed at his wife's excitement, reproving her for making such a noise about the matter." But she would not be appeased, and finally Peire Vidal, fearing that his life was in danger, went beyond the sea, and took the cross under Richard Cœur de Lion. There he distinguished himself by feats of arms, and also wrote very pathetic songs about the kiss he had snatched. At last the Lord Barral, who missed him sadly, prevailed upon his wife to allow him to return in safety to Provence, and even to promise to return in public the kiss he had taken. Then he sent word to Peire Vidal, who returned joyfully, and was most graciously received by Lord Barral and his wife, and the Lady Azalaïs gave him back the kiss he had taken, and he made a famous song about it.

Schlegel says: "Every one talks of the troubadours, and nobody knows anything about them;" but that can hardly be said now, since German scholars have turned their attention that way. These treasure-seekers in the *débris* of MSS., scattered by reformation and revolutions, are constantly unearthing beautiful fragments of the utterances of the first vulgar tongue that ever found expression in literature. The editors, too, of "Romania," Paul Meyer and Gaston de Paris, have spent many summers examining the valuable collections in the public and private libraries of England, and during the winter have given to the world the results of their researches in the pages of their valuable quarterly.

Provence enjoyed almost entire immunity from the ravages and disorders that prevailed in the tenth century; and Languedoc was never invaded like the north of France. The mild Burgundian rule was a peaceful one, and the people dwelt in comparative freedom. Climatic influences too, the southern exposure, helped to ripen that beautiful language, "eldest daughter of the Latin," in which the Provençal poets gave to the world all the Celtic, Frankish, and Arabian legends, of which the air was full in those days. The stories of Arthur and the knights of the round table, of Charlemagne and his peers, first obtained currency through the troubadours. Eschembach, the minnesinger, in his "Titurel and Parceval," expressly acknowledges his indebtedness to the "Provençal Guyot;" and he also criticises freely the Norman French version of "Chrétien of Troyes," showing his familiarity with the "langue d'oil," as well as the "langue d'oc."

William IX., Count of Poitiers, who lived in the eleventh century, is the earliest known troubadour; and he writes in such a polished style that he had evidently found in his language a ready-made instrument, whose "music helped his verses best." Even with our imperfect knowledge of the pronunciation, we can readily understand how the stories of the "Holy Grayle" and the wars against the Saracens, conveyed through such a melodious medium, became popular in Italy, Spain, France, and England. In fact, these versions still embody for us the most complete expression of the religious and political life of the Middle Ages.

It was in Provençal doubtless that Dante's Paolo and Francesca read of Lancelot; and Petrarch and Petrarch's Laura were students of these old romances. Ariosto and Cervantes experienced and transmitted their fascination;

and, in our own language, Chaucer, Shakespeare, Sir Walter Scott, Southey, Tennyson, and the realistic poets of the modern school, have quaffed deep draughts at the sources of French song.

The cradle of art was also the cradle of religious liberty. These great lovers were great haters; and Rome crushed the most fearless, eloquent, and uncompromising upbraiders of priestly corruption in the bloody crusade of the thirteenth century. In so doing, Mother Church imbrued her hands in the blood of her own offspring; for hymns to the Virgin, and legends of the saints in rhyme and assonance, are among the earliest utterances of French poetry. The legends, or "prose" as they were called, were read in the churches till Charlemagne cemented his relations with Rome. Then the story of the Passion and the martyrdom of Stephen were alone retained, since they were to be found in the authorized version of the Scriptures. Some of the sermons quoted by Bartsch, in his "Chrestomathie Provençale," are very artless and simple, particularly the one on the birth and presentation of the Virgin, — the text, as it were, of Titian's picture-poem. A "Confession," bearing date of the eleventh century, gives some idea of the quaintness and earnestness of these early rhymers: —

> O Lord, forgive me, for I trust
> Entirely to Thee.
> What I have done and said and thought,
> All my perversity,
>
> From natal and baptismal hour
> Down to the present day,
> To Thee, High Priest, Almighty God,
> I do bewail alway.

The Evil One has written down,
  To keep me in his power,
The wicked deeds and sinful thoughts
  Of every passing hour.

Sweet Jesus! for Thy Mother's sake,
  Thy pardon I implore,
And by my youthful trespasses
  I will offend no more.

From God, Thy Mother, and from Thee,
  I humbly mercy pray;
For then the devil will be vexed
  Upon the judgment-day.

Oh, keep me, in temptation's hour,
  From every shameful sin.
Dear God, without Thy loving aid
  No soul can enter in.

Sin is so strong, and we are weak,
  And I have faithless grown.
O Lord, in my extreme distress,
  I cling to Thee alone.

Lebeuf found the poem on Boëthius — which is, except the oath of Louis the German, the oldest monument of the French language — in the Benedictine Abbey of Fleury on the Loire, founded in the sixth century. He tells us that in the eleventh century this abbey boasted five thousand students, and each student was required every year to copy two MSS. for the library. Here was found the lost treatise of Cicero on the "Republic." Unfortunately for the interests of literature, one of the Colignys was abbot of Fleury in the sixteenth century, and under his auspices the friends of reform scattered to the winds the treasures of the richest library in France.

Many fell into the hands of the Elector Palatine, and became the nucleus of the library of Heidelberg, and others, purchased by Christina of Sweden, are now in the Vatican. Some of these MSS. contain touching memorials of the transcribers. Here are a few lines found at the end of a beautiful MS. of the eleventh century:—

> To an end our work has come,
> Father, hear our orison!
> Wearily we drop the pen,
> While the brothers chant "Amen."
> It may be that we aimed too high,
> Wanting in humility.
> In the coming judgment-day,
> Help us, Lord, we humbly pray!

The Provençal epic of "Gérard de Roussillon" is a poetical picture of one of the great rebellions which brought about the dissolution of the Frankish monarchy. It belongs to the second part of the Carlovingian romances, the first part comprising the wars of Charlemagne with the Saracens, and the second the revolts of the nobles against that great monarch's descendants. Neither series is much given to love passages, faithful pictures as they are of the anarchy of the Middle Ages; but in "Gérard de Roussillon" they do occur. Gérard himself, and his heroic wife Bertha, are veritable historic personages. Her unwearied devotion to her husband makes her one of the most charming portraitures of the old romances. The circumstances of her marriage are curious, and throw light upon the singular customs of the time; for they are simply related as matters of course, requiring no comment. Charles the Bald, turned into Charles Martel by the poet, loves and marries a lady who appears to be the daughter or near relative of the Emperor of Constantinople. This lady and Gérard have long loved each other; but, not to deprive her of a crown, he consents to her marriage with the Emperor, and resigns himself to take to wife Bertha, sister of his ladylove. Both marriages are solemnized at the same time, and when the hour of parting comes, an extraordinary scene takes place. On the point of separating, perhaps forever, from her friend, the newly made Empress wishes to give him a solemn assurance of her undying tenderness, and is joined to him in a sort of spiritual union. The fragment of this poem in Provençal begins with a description of the marriage with Gérard thus:—

"At the break of day, Gérard led the Queen forth under a tree, and she took with her two counts, friends of hers, and her sister Bertha. 'Wife of the Emperor,' said Gérard, 'what do you think of my taking an inferior in your place?' 'It is most true, my lord, that you have made me an Empress, and that you have married my sister for love of me; but she is also most worthy and noble. Listen to me, Counts Gervais and Bertelais, and you my sister, the confidante of my thoughts, and you, most of all, Jesus my Redeemer! I take you all as sureties and witnesses that with this ring I give my love forever to the Duke Gérard, and make him my knight and seneschal; and I declare before you all that I love him better than my father and my husband, and when I see him go away I cannot help weeping.' Then she placed a ring on his finger. From that time," the narrative continues, "the love of Gérard and the Queen lasted without wrong-doing on either side, nor was there anything between them but tender wishes and secret thoughts."

The story goes on to describe the subsequent quarrels of the Emperor and his haughty vassal. At last Gérard has a price set upon his head, and, with his faithful wife, he is driven to take refuge among the charcoal-burners in the forest of Ardennes. There they live twenty years, and there are many touching passages — one where Gérard and Bertha in their wanderings come to a place where all the able-bodied men have been killed in the wars between him and Charles Martel, and he hears himself cursed by the desolate widows and orphans. At last Bertha persuades her husband to return to the court, and seek the Emperor's pardon, reminding him what a powerful advocate he may expect in her sister; and she gives him back the betrothal ring, which he has thought lost, but which she has kept safely in all their wanderings, and entreats him to make use of it. They reach the court in Holy Week, and on Good Friday evening, when the Empress goes barefooted to the dimly lighted vaulted chapel to hear the "Tenebrae" sung, Gérard draws near and makes himself known. "Then," says our author, "there was no more Good Friday for her; she kissed him one hundred times upon the spot." She asks for her sister, who is not far off, and Gérard tells her all his wife has been to him these many weary years, and says he would have been dead twenty times over if it had not been for her. The Empress sends for a faithful servant, places Gérard and Bertha in safe keeping, tenderly caring for their comfort, and the three spend the whole night in converse. Finally the Empress contrives to make her husband promise not to take vengeance on Gérard, and to restore his estates.

Unlike the troubadours, the Norman French poets

seem to write in complete unconsciousness of the turmoil around them. Here are two specimens of the anonymous romances of the twelfth century: —

On a long, bright day of May,
Home repairing from the court,
Franks from France, in bright array,
Throng the roads in company.
Past the Erembors' domain
Rides Raynaut before the rest;
Never lifting up his eyes,
Never drawing bridle rein.
"O Raynaut, my friend!"

'Tis the lady Erembors;
At the window sitteth she,
On her knees the gorgeousness
Of her bright embroidery.
Far away she sees the throng,
And Raynaut goes riding by.
Pale with passion and with pain,
She must speak, if ne'er again.
"O Raynaut, my friend!"

"My friend Raynaut, there was a time
When close beside my father's towers
You never would have spurred your steed
Without one word from Erembors."
"Disloyal, noble lady: thou
Most faithless art, forgetting me!"
"Sir Raynaut, stay! I will be heard —
I will make known my truth to thee.
A hundred maidens I will bring
And thirty dames on Holy Rood,
To swear I have been true to thee;
Never a man save thee I loved.
Believe me now, and with a kiss
I'll show you what forgiveness is;
O Raynaut, my friend!"

Not in vain the lady pleadeth;
Quickly up the narrow stair
Springs Raynaut, a manly figure:
Light his beard and close-curled hair.
Ne'er in all the land was seen
Gallant of a goodlier mien.
And he comes into the tower,
And he weeps, beholding there,
On a couch all worked with flowers,
Statue still, exceeding fair,
That proud lady Erembors.
Tears of joy and not of pain
Fall when lovers meet again:
"O Raynaut, my friend!"

The following is a more regular, and we might almost say modern, measure ; but how quaint and mediæval is the picture of the knight returning from the quintain, that famous tilting spot of the period!

ROMANCE OF THE TWO SISTERS.

It was eve of Saturday,
And the week was almost done;
Hand in hand the sisters twain
Gaiète and Orriour came
Out to bathe at set of sun.
Breezes blow, the branches move;
Sweet the sleep of those who love.

From the quintain, Childe Gerairs,
Homeward wending, passeth by;
He hath seen and loved Gaiète
At the fountain where they met.
In his strong arms clasped has he
Folded her right tenderly.
Breezes blow, the branches move;
Sweet the sleep of those who love.

"Orriour, when the water's drawn,
Hie thee back into the town.

> Well thou knowest our wonted way,
> Thou mayest go, but I shall stay;
> Here far rather would I be
> With Gerairs who prizeth me."
>
> Weeping, with a bursting heart,
> Orriour has turned away
> All alone, for nevermore
> Gaiète goes with Orriour
> As she went but yesterday.
>
> "Sad the day that I was born,"
> Moaneth Orriour; "woe is me!
> I have left my sister fair
> At the fountain with Gerairs.
> Would I brought her back with me."
>
> Then the knight and maiden went
> By the very shortest way
> To the city. Entering there
> Gaiète married Childe Gerairs
> In a haste brooked no delay.
> Breezes blow, the branches move;
> Sweet the sleep of those who love.

In the South there were many varieties of poems. Novellas were usually tales; but there is one, called "Novas del Hérétic," containing a doctrinal disquisition of a Dominican monk with an Albigensian heretic. Then the elaborate sixtine of Arnaut Daniel imitated by Dante and Petrarch, is truly verse in fetters. Besides these, there are "descorts," "pastorelles," "épîtres," "retröensas," "romances," "sérénades," "aubades," and "ballades." We give a specimen of the last: —

> Fair I am, and much it grieves me
> That my husband does not please me.
> Let me tell you why this sighing:
> Fair I am,

And I want a husband boyish,
Who will frolic when I'm foolish:
    Fair I am.
Should I ever meet my lover,
    Fair I am,
He my passion would discover,
    Fair I am.
But this husband stern and grim,
I am so ashamed of him
That his absence would relieve me.
If he died, it would not grieve me:
    Fair I am.
But of one thing I am sure,
    Fair I am:
Of the friend I loved before,
    Fair I am.
Vainly hoping, I can only
Weep because I am so lonely:
    Fair I am.
Thus I would bespeak you fair,
    Fair I am,
That this ballad far and near
    May be sung.
And those fair ones who do know
Of my love may tell him how
    Fair I am;
That to him my heart is given,
And my hopes this side of heaven:
    Fair I am.

The "tenson" is a dialogue in which two people defend, turn by turn, their respective opinions on some mooted point of love, chivalry, or morals. The question was either left undecided or referred to some court of love, presided over by a noble lady; or else they abided by the decision of a fair and wise arbiter or arbiters chosen by the high contestants themselves. Sometimes it was a satirical, reproachful dialogue, and occasionally it was made the vehicle for the reciprocal accusations of lovers who had quarrelled. For instance, the famous "tenson" of the Countess of Die and Raimbaut, Count of Orange, said to have been imitated from Horace's "Donec gratus eram tibi." They were sometimes called "jeux-partis" and also "tourneymens" or poetical jousts, when more than two took part in the contest. The following is an example: —

Savari de Mauléon, a rich baron of Poitou, loved a noble Gascon lady, the Countess Guillemette de Bénarges, who encouraged also the attentions of two other knights, Elias and Geoffroi de Rudel. One day, when all three were paying their court to her, the coquettish Countess made each one think himself especially favored. She looked tenderly at Geoffroi de Rudel, pressed the hand of Elias, and touched Savari de Mauléon's foot lightly with her own. Neither suspected that his rivals had participated in his privileges; but when they all went away together, Geoffroi and Elias boasted of the favors shown them. Savari listened in silence, and was inclined to think that he still had the advantage over the others. Without naming the Countess, he afterwards referred the question to Hugh de la Bachelleria and Gancelm Faidit. That is the subject of the following tenson or "tourneymen:" —

>Gancelm, a three-part question game
>I now propose to you and Hugh;
>And you may choose and leave to me
>Whichever you prefer to do:
>Three suitors has a lady fair;
>She smiles on all; for when before her
>They all appear to pay their court,
>Each thinks himself the blest adorer.

On one she looks with loving eyes,
The second's hand is softly pressed,
And laughingly her little foot
Has touched the third, as if in jest.
Decide, on judging these aright,
Which one may be the favored knight.

Gancelm Faidit.

My Lord Savari, well you know
That a kind look from loving eyes
Comes from the heart and seeks the heart,
Free from all guile and subtleties.
And so I judge the lady's grace
A hundredfold more given to him
Than to the knight whom grasp of hand
With courteous welcome ushers in.
And as for touching of the foot,
'Tis no love token to my mind :
Most ladies are more serious
When they to loving are inclined.

Hugh de la Bachelleria.

Gancelm, you plead as suits you best;
But I must say I disagree
Entirely with what you say.
The eyes, it always seems to me,
Are meant for public use and show,
Common exchange of feeling, when
A gentle pressure of the hand
Is meant for man, and not for men.
A soft white hand withdrawn from glove,
Given and taken for love's sake,
Is interchange of true regard.
Be sure your friend does not mistake.
To Savari I leave to prove
That pressure of the foot is love.

Savari de Mauléon.

Lord Hugh, since you have left the best,
I take it without more ado.
Touching the foot I shall aver
Is proof of love both warm and true.

That they were merry is a proof
Of being free from craft or guile.
Compared with pressure of the hand,
Or glance of eye, or lady's smile,
How meaning! Cannot Gancelm see
That loving thrives on mystery?

GANCELM FAIDIT.

My Lord, before you criticise
Lord Savari, I marvel much
That you should loftily despise
The sweet, fond looks of ladies' eyes.
They are the faithful messengers,
The trusty envoys of the lover,
Revealing all the heart in fear
Would never venture to discover,
True medium of pure delight;
And many a time, in hours of glee,
You touch a foot in mirthful mood,
Without a thought of coquetry.

HUGH DE LA BACHELLERIA.

Gancelm, you and Mauléon's Lord
Both seem to me at war with love;
And those bright eyes whose cause you plead,
And true as brilliant fain would prove,
Have played the deuce with many a man.
And I should not be overjoyed
If that same lady, false as fair,
In unconcerned frivolity,
Had touched my foot the livelong year —
Worthless to me as smile or tear.
But the warm pressure of the hand,
It is to me a hundredfold
More worth the having. Can the heart
Choose such a faithful messenger
Thus to enact a traitor's part?
Gancelm, I ask for no appeal,
Because I need no advocate.
I have one loyal, loving judge,
And I can well afford to wait.
You two alone have named the three,
So judge for you is not for me.

It is evident that ladies were accustomed to act as judges of these vexed questions. They presided too over the courts of love, where they professed to abide by the code of laws intrusted first to King Arthur.

No troubadour is more justly celebrated than Bertrand de Born, the stormiest spirit of the thirteenth century, and the most turbulent and ungovernable of French barons. He was Lord of Hautefort, an almost impregnable rock fortress in the bishopric of Périgord, and had a thousand men-at-arms at his bidding. He constantly contrived to make trouble between the courts of France, Spain, and England, encouraging the children of Henry II. to rebel against their father. He was the especial friend of the young King Henry, Duke of Guienne, surnamed "Court Mantel," who was crowned during his father's lifetime. Dante calls Bertrand de Born the "new Achitophel of this modern Absalom." After Henry's early death he wrote this elegy or "complainte:"—

LAMENT OF BERTRAND DE BORN FOR THE DEATH OF THE SON OF HENRY II. OF ENGLAND.

> If all the mourning and the tears, the woe,
>   The sorrow, and the sin, the misery
> Could be collected of these troublous times,
>   It would be light to our great grief for thee.
> Young English king! whose fame doth still survive,
>   Bright through thy clouded youth's extreme distress,
> This gloomy world has grown as black as night.
>   We had not wept so did we love thee less.
>
> The jocund soldiery stand dumb with woe;
>   Hushed is the troubadour's, the jongleur's song;
> They both have found in death a mortal foe,
>   Whose fatal grasp on thee has been too strong,

Young English king! whose generous, lavish hand
    Made princes seem like misers. Not for thee
Can sorrow half enough this stricken land:
    Not with the tears of the whole century.

O potent Death! fell cause of all our woe!
    Thou art vainglorious to have won for thee
The noblest knight that trod this earth below,
    Light of our eyes, the flower of chivalry!
Young English king! I would to God thy name
    Were yet a rallying cry, and those who shame
Brave men, whose death would be a great relief,
    Were gone instead; then were no cause of grief.
Degenerate age! so full of mortal woe;
    If love be absent, joy is all a cheat.
Since all things end in suffering, every day
    Is worth less than its fellows. At thy feet,
Young English king! the valiant and the brave,
    The world may sit in wonder; for they know,
Now that thy loving heart is in the grave,
    None live like thee to cheer this world below.

To Him who came unto this world of woe,
    And brought salvation to the sons of men
By His own death, to our liege Lord we bow,
    And here implore for the young English king
An unconditioned pardon and a place
    High in the ranks of the redeemed, with men,
Brothers in arms for nobleness and grace,
    Where never wrath or weeping comes again.

We find the following anecdote in Raynouard's "Biographies des Troubadours." King Henry of England besieged Bertrand de Born in his castle of Hautefort, and brought down all his engines of war against him; for he wished him great harm because he believed that Bertrand had incited the young king, his son, to rebellion against his father. And they razed the walls and took the castle, and Bertrand and all his men were brought prisoners before the tent of King Henry. The King received him very coldly, and said scornfully : "Bertrand, I have heard that you said that you never needed to use more than half the wit at your command. Now, methinks, you are at fault." "I did say so, and you speak truly, my lord," answered Bertrand. "Now," said the King, "I should say you were at your wit's end." "My lord," said Bertrand, "I am indeed most destitute." "How is that?" said the King. "My lord," said Bertrand, "the day when the young king, your valiant son, died, I lost all I had in the world, and the use of all my faculties." And when the King heard what Bertrand said the tears streamed from his eyes, and he felt such a pain in his heart that he swooned away. And when he came to himself he cried out weeping, "Lord Bertrand, Lord Bertrand! you are right; it is most true that you lost all in losing my son, for he loved you better than any man in the world; and for his sake I restore to you your freedom, and your lands, and your castle, and your place in my favor; and I give you, moreover, five hundred marks of silver to make amends for the injury you have received at my hands." Then Bertrand fell at his feet and returned him thanks, and the King went away with his whole army.

We give below a famous "sirvente" of Bertrand de Born. The sirventes were generally satirical or declamatory political poems, and were occasionally abusive of persons in power. "Papiol" was the favorite *jongleur* of Bertrand, and "Yes and No" was his name for Richard Cœur de Lion : —

> I like it well, the sweet spring-time,
> That brings the leaves and flowers,
> And I like well the carolling

Of birds, their songs re-echoing
Through groves and leafy bowers.
I like it well when, on the mead,
Tents and pavilions shine;
And in my very heart I like,
When horse and horseman armed to strike,
Stand in a gleaming line.

I like it well when raiders swoop
Down on the herdsmen flying.
I like it when the angry guard
In hot pursuit is hieing.
Great joy it bringeth me
When strongholds old, by armies bold,
Beleaguered I can see;
When toppling walls uprooted fall,
And on the shore I see,
Beyond the ditch and palisades,
The watchful enemy.

A good knight also pleaseth me,
When first he rides into the fray,
With horse in armor fearlessly;
For well he shows his men the way,
With such undaunted bravery,
That, when they come upon the field,
Each man would rather die than yield,
And follows willingly;
For who would be esteemed a knight
Must deal hard blows in many a fight.

Lances and swords, gay waving crests,
Surge in the battle's van,
And shields dismantled and pierced through.
The blows are neither faint nor few,
Well dealt by knights of valor true,
Contending man to man.
And frightened horses loose are flying,
Charging among the dead and dying.
No count of lineage high
But feels, rejoicing in the strife,
Far better death than shameful life.

I tell you, better far than sleep,
Or sounds of revelry,
I like to hear the shout ring clear,
" Have at them, till they flee!"
Impatiently the horses neigh,
'Neath shelter of the wood,
While dying men choke up the moat:
Little and great are there afloat,
The grass all stained with blood;
And knights upon the ground are dying —
Transfixed with spears where they are lying.
Gallant nobles yield as pledges
Castles, towns, and villages.
Ere you go to war anew,
Papiol, I bid thee go
Straightway back to "Yes and No."
Say, from one who understands,
Peace hangs heavy on our hands.

It will be seen that the troubadours were not all of lowly birth. When the aristocracies of rank and genius were united, they made the ideal man of the time. Richard Cœur de Lion was a troubadour of no mean pretension. The following lament, written by him in captivity, when he was thrown into prison on his return from the crusades by the Emperor of Germany, exists in Norman French and also in Provençal : —

A man in prison never sings so well
As though he were not in captivity;
But still for comfort he may make a song.
My friends, though many, are but scant in gifts.
It is a shame, for want of ransom here,
Two years I am a prisoner.

They know it well, my liegemen and my barons,
The English, Normans, Poitevins, and Gascons,
That there is none so poor among them all
Whom I would leave in chains for lack of gold.
I do not say it as an accusation,
But here I still am prisoner.

I hold it now to be a certain truth,
Dead men and prisoners have no kith or kin.
For want of money that they leave me here
Is bad for me, but worse it is for them.
When I am dead they will be greatly blamed,
I was so long a prisoner.

It is not strange that I am sad at heart;
For my liege-lord doth keep my land in turmoil.
If he bethought him of our mutual oath,
It is most certain that no longer here
Could I be held a prisoner.

They know it well, the Anjou and Touraine,
Who bear them bravely in their stalwart youth,
That far from them I still am tethered here.
They used to love me; now they love me not.
No more these plains are famed for feats of arms,
While I am held a prisoner.

My friends, whom loving once I always love,
Those of Cahors and those of Percherain,
Tell me, my song, are they not true to me?
Was I to them e'er false or hollow-hearted?
If they war on me, they are worse than wicked,
So long as I am prisoner.

My countess-sister, your liege-lord in durance
Salutes you, praying you may be in keeping
Of Him to whom I make my last appeal,
By whose will I am prisoner.
I do not mean by this the dame of Chartres, mother of Louis.

The student of manners and customs, no less than the philologist, finds much to interest him in these almost unexplored regions of old French poetry. That we have hitherto neglected the study is not so strange as that modern French authors should contentedly date from the age of Louis XIV., ignoring their inheritance of the richest, sweetest literature of the Middle Ages.

www.ingramcontent.com/pod-product-compliance
Lightning Source LLC
Chambersburg PA
CBHW030333170426
43202CB00010B/1117